BADGES ON BATTLEDRESS

Badges on Battledress

POST-WAR
FORMATION SIGNS
and
RANK AND REGIMENTAL BADGES

by

LIEUT.-COLONEL HOWARD N. COLE,
O.B.E., T.D., F.R.Hist.S.
President of the Military Heraldry Society

The Naval & Military Press Ltd

Published by

The Naval & Military Press Ltd
Unit 5 Riverside, Brambleside
Bellbrook Industrial Estate
Uckfield, East Sussex
TN22 1QQ England

Tel: +44 (0)1825 749494

www.naval-military-press.com
www.nmarchive.com

In reprinting in facsimile from the original, any imperfections are inevitably reproduced and the quality may fall short of modern type and cartographic standards.

CONTENTS

	page
Formation Signs Today	1
Post-War Formation Badges	5
Home Commands	12
Overseas Commands	17
British Army of the Rhine	25
Home Districts and Garrisons	31
Overseas Areas, Districts and Garrisons	43
Regular Army Formations (Corps and Divisions)	52
Regular Army Infantry Brigades	63
Airborne Forces	71
Training Brigade Groups	72
Royal Artillery Formations (Regular Army)	78
Royal Engineer Units (Regular Army)	80
Royal Signals Units (Regular Army)	82
R.A.S.C. Units (Regular Army)	83
Territorial Army Formations	85
Territorial Army Divisions	86
Armoured Brigades (T.A.)	96
Infantry Brigades (T.A.)	98
Royal Artillery Formations (Territorial Army)	102
Royal Engineer Formations (Territorial Army)	112
Canadian Army	116
Australian Army	121
Regimental Badges and Shoulder Flashes	128

CONTENTS—continued

	page
Miscellaneous Badges	157
The Wearing of Badges on Battledress	161
Tartan Flashes and Patches worn by Scottish Regiments	167
Officers' Rank Badges	168
Distinguishing Colouring of Background of Worsted Badges of Rank worn on Battledress	171
Gorget Patches	173
Warrant Officers' Rank Badges	176
Non-Commissioned Officers' Rank Badges	180
Badges of Appointments	187
Instructors' Badges	189
Tradesmen's Badges	192
Skill-at-Arms Badges	196
Abbreviations	201

ILLUSTRATIONS

Badges on Battledress ... ... *Frontispiece*

	page
The formation sign of Aldershot District in use on a direction board	203
On Active Service—Korea—Officers of the Middlesex Regiment and the Argyll and Sutherland Highlanders wearing the badge of the 40th Division	204
The formation sign in use as a vehicle marking. (The sign depicted on this vehicle is that of 100 A.G.R.A. (A.A.) (T.A.))	205
The Western Union Standard which incorporates the badges of the H.Q. Western Europe Commanders-in-Chief	206
The formation sign of the 52nd (Lowland) Division (T.A.) in use on a Brigade Pennant	207
The Royal Artillery Standard incorporating a Formation Badge	208
The badges of S.H.A.P.E. and the 1st Canadian Rifle Battalion	209
Embroidered badges—Ordnance issues—The East Anglian Brigade and East and West Ridings Area	210
Printed badges—Ordnance issues—East Africa Command and the 40th Division	211
The two types of formation badges as worn by the 42nd (Lancashire) Division (T.A.)	212
Formation badges reproduced on Greeting Cards ...	213
Formation badges reproduced on medals	214
Formation badges incorporated into ties	215
The Arms of the Board of Ordnance	216
Rank, Skill-at-Arms and Tradesmen's badges ...	217

PREFACE TO THE FIRST EDITION

WHEN, during the war, I first started to collect formation badges I had no idea that the numbers would reach the figure that forms my collection today; and when, shortly after V J Day, I set myself the task of recording the detail of the many designs, collating information regarding their symbolism and origin, and recording brief histories of the formations which bore them, I did so under the impression that, as was the case after the 1914-18 War, such badges would soon cease to be worn, and that it was only a matter of time before they became but of historical interest.

This, however, was not the case. The Army, Corps and Divisional signs of the 1914-18 War soon fell into disuse, but not so those of the late war. The formation badges of 1939-45 continued to be worn until the release of personnel led to the disbandment of most of the war-time formations. Whilst this process was reducing our Army in numbers it also led to reorganization, on the redistribution of our forces, and the establishment of new formations to meet post-war requirements. Instead of formation badges falling into disuse, new badges were introduced, old badges modified and changed; and so the collector had fresh fields to explore. I continued to collect each new badge as soon as I discovered its introduction, and so the war-time collection grew. Had the formation badge come to stay? Was it in future to be an accepted military custom? Would it be authorized as part of the dress of the Army in time of peace? These questions were recently answered by the publication of an Army Council Instruction giving approval to the retention of existing badges and the adoption of new designs.

I had been working on a revised edition of my book, "Heraldry in War—Formation Badges, 1939-45," and in view of the many new badges introduced since the war was faced with the problem of where to stop. No one can say that the new badges introduced in the last eighteen months could be classified as "war-time" badges under the title "Heraldry in War." Was it best to change the title of my first book on the subject, produce a post-war appendix, or start again from, say, 1946? I decided on the last course.

"Heraldry in War" was originally intended to cover only the formation badges worn during the war years, but in the second edition of that book I did include a few badges introduced since V J Day.

My self-imposed terms of reference for this smaller work were to record all formation badges worn today. In consequence there is an overlap in so far as certain formations are concerned, which, by force of circumstances, are mentioned and illustrated in both "Heraldry in War" and in this book. These are the few new badges, introduced in 1946, and the war-time badges which continue to be worn by the post-war successors to the war-time formations. In addition, however, this book covers fifty-nine new badges introduced in the last two years.

With the object of simplicity and in order to modify production costs I have adhered to black-and-white sketches of the badges. In order to avoid complexity in the sketches, especially in the smaller designs, I have not used the conventional heraldic "hatchings" to denote tincture which were introduced early in the seventeenth century for use in engravings and in line drawings. The colouring of each badge is described in the text.

New badges are still being introduced and I cannot hope to have included all the badges that have been adopted since the war; therefore this small book does not aspire to being the complete authority; but, knowing of the considerable interest that exists in this modern form of military heraldry, I have been tempted to record now this collection of post-war formation badges which it is hoped will be of interest to many who made war-time collections and to those who desire a handy reference book of the formation badges worn today. I shall be most grateful to any reader who has knowledge of any badges not included in these pages if he would care to help in adding to this information by sending details to me (c/o the Publishers), with, if possible, a specimen or sketch. I will gladly acknowledge his help in any future edition, should one be warranted.

I am already indebted to the many formation Commanders and their Staff Officers who have assisted me by sending me information and samples of the new badges described in the following pages, and I take this opportunity of recording my appreciation of their help and interest.

ALDERSHOT, HOWARD N. COLE.
February, 1949.

PREFACE TO THE SECOND EDITION

IT is but two years since the publication of the first edition of this record of the formation badges adopted or reintroduced in the post-war years. It was then that I wrote "the formation sign has its place in peace as much as it had in war," and this has been borne out by the continuance of the practice of wearing these badges (authorized in 1948 for wear in both peace and war) and the introduction of many new designs. The title of the book has perhaps become more appropriate too, for once again British troops have gone into action, wearing formation badges on their battledress, in Korea and in Malaya. The Yellow Cock of the 40th Division, worn by the 27th British Commonwealth Brigade, and the White Circle of the 29th Brigade have added to the glory and prestige of the British Army in the hard fighting with the United Nations forces on the rugged Korean battlefields, whilst the green, clinging jungles of Malaya have seen the familiar signs of the 2nd Guards Brigade, the Gurkha Brigade, and the other formations faced with the task of ridding Malaya of the bandit forces.

I have been able to include in this edition descriptions and illustrations of forty-nine entirely new badges introduced in the past two and a half years, and fourteen wartime badges which have been reintroduced, together with references to the new formation badges adopted by the Australian Military Forces and those of the Dominion of

Canada. I have also extended the field of the work to include reference to and detail of a number of purely regimental badges and flashes which have been retained since the late war or adopted in recent years. These are now included in a special section of the book, for they do come within the scope of the title, since they are "Badges on Battledress."

I take this opportunity of recording my appreciation of the help I have received from those who have sent me badges, drawings and descriptive detail which I have used in the compilation of this edition, and I wish to thank:

The Director of Staff Duties of the Army Headquarters of the Australian Military Forces for his great assistance in providing the material for the section devoted to the new formation badges adopted by the Australian formations; Brigadier L. C. Aitken, O.B.E.; Brigadier F. W. Rice; Brigadier E. F. Sheehan, Australian Military Forces; Brigadier G. A. Viner, O.B.E.; Colonel R. F. Monaghan, Australian Military Forces; Lieut.-Colonel A. E. C. Bredin, D.S.O., M.C., The Dorset Regiment; Lieut.-Colonel R. Chandler, D.S.O.; Lieut.-Colonel J. A. d'Avigdor-Goldsmid, M.C., 4th/7th Royal Dragoon Guards; Lieut.-Colonel J. A. Cooke, 9th Queen's Royal Lancers; Lieut.-Colonel J. R. D. Galloway, O.B.E., R.A.; Lieut.-Colonel J. F. W. Jackson; Lieut.-Colonel A. G. L. Maclean, C.B.E.; Lieut.-Colonel J. A. E. P. Richardson; Lieut.-Colonel D. Swinburn, O.B.E.; Lieut.-Colonel J. R. Thatcher; Major R. E. Austin, Duke of Wellington's Regiment; Major C. F. F. Anderson, R.A.; Major R. Butler, R.A.; Major J. Bruce, The Royal Scots; Major D. R. Carroll, R.E.; Major A. J. W. Grubb, R.A.; Major J. R. Gutch, R.A.; Major K. B. Langdon, R.A.; Major A. E. Ruddle, R.A.; Major P. S. Sandilands, D.S.O., Royal Scots Fusiliers; Captain H. Ashton, R.A.; Captain F. H. Blake; Captain W. A. Ewbank, M.C., R.E.; Captain A. W. Gage, 13th/18th Hussars; Captain A. B. Houston, Fife and Forfar Yeomanry; Captain G. H. Hodgkinson, Royal Gloucestershire Hussars; Captain (Q.M.) J. W. Johnson, R.A.; Captain J. P. Sanders; Captain G. Williams, R.A.; Captain J. Waring, D.L.I.; Captain J. B. Wilson; A. H. Patterson, Esq., of Messrs. W. Anderson & Sons Ltd., Edinburgh; Corporal G. Campbell, Royal Signals.

There is still a continued and even increasing interest in the study of these badges. A new and wide field has been opened up to the collector, and many interesting private collections now exist, built up by those who have found in the formation badge scope for research which at the same time provides a fascinating study. This has led to the recent establishment of The Military Heraldry Society on the initiative of Captain J. Waring of the Durham Light Infantry, which honoured me by inviting me to accept its Presidency. The Society has been formed with the objects of promoting and fostering a general interest in the study of British and foreign military formation signs, and to assist collectors in their researches.

It has given me much pleasure to be associated with this Society, which has adopted these objects for its *raison d'être*, for I have always been convinced of the importance of the formation sign—not only the purpose for which it was originally introduced but the *esprit de corps* which has been created within formations, and which can, to a great extent, be attributed to the symbolism of the badge of identification, and the comradeship between those who wear the badges by which they are proud to identify themselves with their particular formation.

HOWARD N. COLE.

TONGHAM,
  September, 1951.

PREFACE TO THE THIRD EDITION

THE subject of "Badges on Battledress" is one which, it is now safe to say, will never reach finality. In like manner as uniforms and regimental badges and distinctions are altered, amended and added to, as time goes by, so constant revision is necessary in a reference book of this nature.

In the year that has passed since the publication of the second, revised and enlarged, edition, eighteen new badges have made their appearance, and three existing badges have, in some degree, been altered in style of design. In addition to which, through research, and contact with a wide circle of Service friends and acquaintances, I have gathered information regarding twelve additional regimental badges and flashes. This new material has, perforce, called for a third edition of this book now that a reprint has become necessary.

There is still a growing interest in the study of formation badges, of their composition, significance and origin, and this obtains not only among serving personnel and those interested in general with matters military, but among the increasing number of collectors, for the collection of these badges has become an interesting and absorbing hobby. Collections take numerous forms, from the carefully preserved and catalogued collections of original badges to even cushion covers and bedspreads (as I have seen) covered with badges stitched closely together to form an attractive kaleidoscope of colour. It is, however, in collections in the former category that the real military interest lies, and much good work in the promotion of, and fostering, a general interest in the study of these badges has been, and is being, constantly carried out by the Military Heraldry Society.

The changes and additions which are continually taking place add zest to the fascinating hobby of collecting these badges, and of gleaning information on the choice of design and the reasons for their adoption. There is, of course, much wider scope for the enthusiastic collector than may be imagined, for the formation badge has now become an almost universal distinguishing badge on the uniforms of the United Nations Forces. "Shoulder Insignia" (*i.e.*, formation badges) of the American Army alone give a very wide field for the ambitious collector. During the late war there were some three hundred badges in use by the U.S. Army and Air Force, and many have been added since 1945. The war in Korea has resulted in the introduction of numerous new badges, not only in the American Army but for the South Korean forces, and all the Allied contingents serving with the U.N.O. Forces in the theatre of operations.*

In the case of some of the smaller contingents, Allied badges are worn, and in Brussels earlier this year I saw two Infantry N.C.Os. of the Belgian Army wearing on their sleeves the badges of both the 29th British Infantry Brigade and the 3rd American Division.

The scope of this book, eventually, may well be enlarged to give a comprehensive survey of all the Allied badges which have been worn in the war in Korea, but at the

---

* Among the numerous distinguishing shoulder/sleeve badges, apart from the British and American formations, now being worn in Korea, are those of: The Columbian, French, Indian, Swedish, Thailand and Turkish Contingents; the Danish Ambulance Unit; 60th Indian Field Ambulance; and the 20th Bn. Combat Team, Philippine Expeditionary Force, together with some 24 badges adopted by South Korean Units.

present time there are difficulties in collecting detailed and accurate information, and so I have adhered to my original intention of keeping this book at present as one of easy reference to the badges on the battledress of the British and Commonwealth Armies.

The formation sign recalls nostalgic memories, as is evidenced by the popularity of wall plaques, book ends and pipe racks bearing the well-remembered badges, and the recent introduction of ties with small reproductions of the badges of the famous formations. Ex-members of those Armies, Corps, and Divisions are pleased and proud to be able to wear in their daily work these reminders of their service, and they are worn with the same pride with which the regimental, school, and club tie has been worn for years.

Perhaps the time is not too distant when the use of the formation badge might take on an even wider meaning and significance. What better than to extend its use to an official Divisional "Colour," or Standard (or Guidon for Armoured Divisions) with the badge embroidered in the centre, and surrounded by the formation's battle honours such as hitherto have only been granted to H.M. Ships and Regiments?

The formation today has a wider appeal to *esprit de corps*. It has its own traditions of service in battle in two World Wars (or one could go back to the Numbered Divisions of the Peninsular, Crimea and South African Wars), and tradition builds *esprit de corps*, which in turn breeds discipline and discipline leads to efficient fighting formations.

There is a trend today among ex-soldiers to place loyalty to a formation above that to Regiment or Corps. The regimental spirit, especially in the Infantry, has always been strong; it still is and will always be so. But how often does one hear, in answer to a question concerning the war service of an individual, "I was with the Eighth Army," or "I was in the 11th Armoured"? The formation spirit, especially in war, is of a high order, of which the outward sign is, of course, the formation badge.

The formation badge continues to have its place in the military life of the nation. The use of these badges increases, and they become more familiar as time goes by, not only by their continued wear on battledress, but by their use when reproduced as vehicle markings; on flags and pennants; on inter-unit and formation trophies; on stationery and Christmas cards; on printed orders, programmes and notices; on directional signs and in many other ways. Some badges lend themselves to unique methods of use. In Rhine Army this spring I saw the cross keys of the 2nd Infantry Division cast in brass and used as car badges on the bonnets of military vehicles; whilst high up on the roof, above the main entrance of the cinema of the Rhine Centre at Dusseldorf, were the two large crossed keys of the Divisional badge.*
At the Hook of Holland I saw the Rhine Army leave and duty train draw in, together with that from Austria; on the rolling stock were painted the badges of Rhine Army, and the famous war-time badge of the Eighth Army—now worn by British Troops in Austria. And so, these two famous badges are seen today on the main railroads of the *Grande Expresses Europeens* along the routes which, in their time, have seen British formations marching forward on the roads to victory.

As with previous editions, I have had the co-operation

---
* See page 56.

and help of many to whom I have written to seek information, and to confirm detail of new formation and regimental badges, and I now record my appreciation of their assistance. I wish to thank:

Captain J. H. Waring, the founder and Hon. Secretary of the Military Heraldry Society; Colonel H. E. M. Cotton, O.B.E.; Colonel R. P. Freeman-Taylor; Colonel A. M. Man, D.S.O., O.B.E.; Colonel A. H. M. Morris, D.S.O., M.C., G.M.; Colonel J. Radford, O.B.E.; Lieut.-Colonel R. A. Cook, R.A.; Lieut.-Colonel C. V. Halden, M.B.E., T.D.; Major J. St. J. Baxter, R.E.; Major P. R. Barrass; Major A. B. Briggs; Major R. C. Clarke (The Dorset Regiment); Major J. Davidson; Major G. W. H. King; Major D. I. A. McKechnie, R.A.; Major O. F. Newton Dunn (The Wiltshire Regiment); Major E. W. D. Steel, R.A.; Captain A. G. Binley, R.A.O.C.; Captain E. J. Marshall, R.A.; W.O.I (S.S.M.) C. J. H. Brenchley, R.A.S.C.; and also Mr. R. A. Garratt, of Messrs. F. Phillips of Aldershot, the manufacturers of the medals reproduced on page 214; and Mr. D. Alston, of Messrs. Welch, Margetson & Co., Ltd., the manufacturers of the ties illustrated on page 215.

The range of interest in badges has, in this edition, been increased by the inclusion of the section dealing with badges of rank, appointments and proficiency, and also tradesmen's badges. It was felt the addition of this material would give the work added interest as a book of reference and make it fully comprehensive of its subject; for, although it was originally intended that it should be a record of formation and regimental badges worn since the late war, its title did give the necessary scope to include this new section, for are not these, too, Badges on Battledress?

HOWARD N. COLE.

TONGHAM,
October, 1952.

INDEX TO FORMATIONS

	page
The War Office	5
War Office Controlled Units	7
Military Staff, Ministry of Supply	8
Supreme Headquarters Allied Powers Europe (SHAPE)	9
Headquarters Allied Land Forces Central Europe	10
H.Q., Western Europe Commanders-in-Chief	11

Home Commands

Northern Command	12
Western Command	13
Eastern Command	13
Southern Command	14
Scottish Command	15
Anti-Aircraft Command	15

Overseas Commands

Middle East Land Forces	17
Far East Land Forces	18
H.Q. British Troops in Egypt and Mediterranean Command	19
Malaya Command	19
East Africa Command	20
West Africa Command	20
H.Q. Land Forces Hong Kong	21
British Commonwealth Forces, Korea	22
H.Q. British Troops in Palestine	22
British Element Trieste Force	23
British Troops in France	24
British Troops in Austria	24

British Army of the Rhine

	page
H.Q. British Army of the Rhine	25
Rhine Army Troops	25
British Troops, Berlin	26
School of Artillery, B.A.O.R.	27
Engineer Training Establishment, B.A.O.R.	27
R.A.C. Training Centre, B.A.O.R.	28
Rhine Army Training Centre	28
Control Commission, Germany	29
Hanover District	29
Hamburg District	30
Rhine District	30
Aquatic Training School	30

Home Districts and Garrisons

London District	31
Northern Ireland District	31
Highland District	32
Lowland District	32
Aldershot District	33
South-Western District	34
Salisbury Plain District	35
Home Counties District	36
East Anglian District	36
North-Western District	37
Mid-Western District	37
Northumbrian District	38
North-Midland District	39
East and West Ridings Area	39
Catterick Garrison	40
Solent Garrison	41
Shoeburyness Garrison	42

Overseas Areas, Districts and Garrisons

	page
1st Infantry Division District, M.E.L.F.	43
Tripolitania District	43
Cyrenaica District	44
Eritrea District	44
Cyprus District	45
Canal South District, M.E.L.F.	46
Canal North District, M.E.L.F.	46
Caribbean Area	47
Singapore District	48
Gold Coast District	49
Nigeria District	49
Sierra Leone and Gambia District	49
Malta Garrison	50
Gibraltar Garrison	50
Ceylon Garrison	51
Gaza Sub-District	51

Regular Army Formations

1st Corps	52
6th Armoured Division	52
7th Armoured Division	53
11th Armoured Division	53
1st Infantry Division	54
Royal Artillery, 1st Infantry Division	55
Royal Signals, 1st Infantry Division	55
Royal Army Service Corps, 1st Infantry Division	55
2nd Infantry Division	56
3rd Infantry Division	57
40th Division	58
No. 1 Commonwealth Division	59
17th Gurkha Division	62
25th Armoured Brigade	62

Infantry Brigades

	page
2nd Guards Brigade	63
17th Infantry Brigade	64
18th Infantry Brigade	65
23rd British Brigade Group	65
24th Infantry Brigade	65
25th Independent Infantry Brigade	66
27th Infantry Brigade	67
29th Infantry Brigade	68
29th British Brigade Group	68
31st Independent Infantry Brigade	69
72nd British Brigade Group	70

Airborne Forces . . . 71

Training Brigade Groups

Yorkshire and Northumberland Group	72
East Anglian Brigade	73
Mercian Group	73
Wessex Group	74
Lancastrian Group	75
Home Counties Group	76
North Irish Group	76
Midland Group	77
"Greenjackets" Group	77

Royal Artillery Formations (Regular Army)

2nd A.G.R.A.	78
3rd A.G.R.A.	78
5th A.G.R.A. (A.A.)	79
18th Training Brigade, R.A.	79

Royal Engineers (Regular Army)

Fortress Engineers, Gibraltar	80
Bomb Disposal Units, R.E.	80
Transportation Units, R.E. (S.R.)	81

Royal Signals (Regular Army)

	page
Air Formation Signals	82
W.R.A.C. Signals Personnel	82

R.A.S.C. Units (Regular Army)

Army Fire Service, R.A.S.C.	83
Air Despatch Group, R.A.S.C.	83
War Department Fleet, R.A.S.C.	84

Territorial Army Formations

Army Troops (T.A.)	85
21st (Northern) Corps	85
23rd (Southern) Corps	86

Territorial Army Divisions

42nd (Lancashire) Division (T.A.)	87
43rd (Wessex) Division (T.A.)	88
44th (Home Counties) Division (T.A.)	89
49th (West Riding and Midland) Armoured Division (T.A.)	90
50th (Northumbrian) Division (T.A.)	90
51st (Highland) Division (T.A.)	91
52nd (Lowland) Division (T.A.)	92
53rd (Welsh) Division (T.A.)	93
56th (London) Armoured Division (T.A.)	94

Armoured Brigades (T.A.)

9th Independent Armoured Brigade (T.A.)	99
23rd Independent Armoured Brigade (T.A.)	96
30th (Lowlands) Independent Armoured Brigade (T.A.)	97

Infantry Brigades (T.A.)

107th (Ulster) Independent Brigade Group (T.A.)	98
161st Independent Infantry Brigade Group (T.A.)	99
162nd Independent Infantry Brigade Group (T.A.)	100
264th (Scottish) Beach Brigade (T.A.)	101

Royal Artillery Formations (T.A.)

	page
84th A.G.R.A. (T.A.)	102
85th A.G.R.A. (T.A.)	103
86th A.G.R.A. (T.A.)	103
87th A.G.R.A. (Field) (T.A.)	104
88th A.G.R.A. (Field) (T.A.)	104
89th A.G.R.A. (Field) (T.A.)	105
90th A.G.R.A. (Field) (T.A.)	105
91st A.G.R.A. (Field) (T.A.)	106
92nd A.G.R.A. (A.A.) (T.A.)	106
93rd A.G.R.A. (T.A.)	107
94th A.G.R.A. (A.A.) (T.A.)	107
95th A.G.R.A. (A.A.) (T.A.)	108
96th A.G.R.A. (A.A.) (T.A.)	108
97th A.G.R.A. (A.A.) (T.A.)	109
100th A.G.R.A. (A.A.) (T.A.)	109
101st Coast Brigade R.A. (T.A.)	110
102nd Coast Brigade R.A. (T.A.)	110
104th Coast Brigade R.A. (T.A.)	110
105th Coast Brigade R.A. (T.A.)	111

Royal Engineer Formations (T.A.)

21st Engineer Group (T.A.)	112
22nd Engineer Group (T.A.)	112
23rd Engineer Group (T.A.)	113
24th Engineer Group (T.A.)	113
25th Engineer Group (T.A.)	114
26th Engineer Group (T.A.)	115
27th Engineer Group (T.A.)	115

Canadian Army

25th Canadian Infantry Brigade	116
27th Canadian Infantry Brigade	117

	page
1st Canadian Infantry Battalion	118
1st Canadian Highland Battalion	119
1st Canadian Rifle Battalion	120

Australian Army

Army Headquarters (Australia)	122
Northern Command (Queensland)	122
Northern Territory Command	122
Central Command (South Australia)	123
Eastern Command (New South Wales)	123
Western Command	123
3rd Military District (Victoria)	124
Tasmania Command	124
2nd Infantry Division	124
3rd Infantry Division	125
1st Infantry Brigade Group	125
11th Infantry Brigade	125
13th Infantry Brigade	126
1st Armoured Brigade	126
2nd Armoured Brigade	126
G.H.Q. Pakistan	127
Hong Kong Defence Force	127
The King's Own Malta Regiment	127

Regimental Badges and Shoulder Flashes

Royal Armoured Corps	129
Royal Armoured Corps Training Regiments	130
4th/7th Royal Dragoon Guards	131
9th Queen's Royal Lancers	132
13th/18th Royal Hussars (Queen Mary's Own)	133
14th/20th King's Hussars	133
Royal Tank Regiment	134
Royal Gloucestershire Hussars	135
Fife and Forfar Yeomanry	135

	page
79th Heavy Anti-Aircraft Regiment, R.A.	136
24th H.A.A. Regiment, R.A.	137
297th (Kent Yeomanry) L.A.A. Regiment, R.A. (T.A.)	138
402nd Light Regiment, R.A. (Argyll and Sutherland Highlanders) (T.A.)	139
515th (Isle of Man) L.A.A. Regiment, R.A. (T.A.)	140
556th (East Lancashire) H.A.A. Regiment, R.A. (T.A.)	141
573rd (Mixed) H.A.A. Regiment, R.A. (T.A.) (The King's Regiment)	142
575th (Sherwood Foresters) L.A.A. Regiment, R.A. (T.A.)	143
576th (Mixed) L.A.A./S.L. Regiment, R.A. (T.A.)	144
580th L.A.A Regiment, R.A. (T.A.)	144
587th L.A.A. Regiment, R.A. (T.A.) (Queen's Edinburgh Royal Scots)	145
602nd H.A.A. (Welch) Regiment, R.A. (T.A.)	146
629th L.A.A. Regiment, R.A. (T.A.)	146
Tyne Electrical Engineers	147
23rd Corps Signal Regiment, Royal Signals (T.A.)	148
Suffolk Regiment	149
Bedfordshire and Hertfordshire Regiment	149
Royal Scots Fusiliers	150
Border Regiment	151
South Staffordshire Regiment	152
Northamptonshire Regiment	152
Wiltshire Regiment	153
Glider Pilot Regiment	153
21st S.A.S. Regiment (Artists) (T.A.)	155
The Malayan Scouts	156

Miscellaneous Badges

Specialized Armour Training Establishment, R.A.C.	157
Army Mechanical Transport School	158
Army Mechanized Demonstration Column	158
British Military Mission to Greece	159
British Service Mission to Burma	159
Danish Brigade Group	160

FORMATION SIGNS TODAY

WITHIN two years of the cessation of hostilities after the 1914-18 War the Army Corps and Divisional Signs which had been introduced into the Army during the war years had fallen into disuse, and had ceased to be worn by the post-war Regular Army.

Between the wars these war-time Divisional Signs were worn by only five of the Territorial Army Divisions—the 47th (2nd London) until it was disbanded in 1935,* the 49th (West Riding), the 51st (Highland), 52nd (Lowland), and the 55th (West Lancashire) Divisions.

During the 1939-45 War, formation signs (redesignated "Formation badges" in 1941†) were universally adopted, being reintroduced in 1940,‡ and more widely used than had been the case in the 1914-18 War, for their use was extended to Home Commands and Districts, Overseas Commands, Districts, Garrison and Sub-Areas, and to Training Establishments and Administrative Units. Over five hundred such badges worn by British, Dominion, Indian and Colonial troops have been recorded.

The formation badge played an important role in war as a distinctive sign, and as a means of promoting *esprit de corps*. That the value of these badges has been appreciated on these two counts alone is proved by the fact that six and a half

---
* Re-formed in 1939.
† Army Council Instructions Nos. 1118 and 1553 of 1940.
‡ Army Council Instruction No. 2587 of 1941.

years after V J Day these badges are still being worn, and there has been a steady rate of introduction of new badges during that period. It would now appear that the formation badge has come to stay as a permanent feature of Army dress and that in the future these badges will be worn by the British Army in both peace and war. In September, 1948, War Office announced* that it had been decided that formation badges may continue to be worn by all formations of the Regular and Territorial Armies, and in consequence, especially in the Territorial Army, this has led to the re-adoption of the now famed war-time badges and the introduction of many new and appropriate designs.

Designs of new badges are initiated by formation Commanders, and in order to avoid duplication are submitted to the War Office† for approval. Designs, once approved, cannot be altered without War Office authority. The badges are a free issue to all ranks, but in the interests of economy printed badges are generally provided. More expensive embroidered badges may be purchased privately by individuals and worn at the discretion of the formation Commanders. Formation badges are provided for the Territorial Army under the same conditions as laid down for the Regular Army.

Formation badges are worn‡ at the top of each sleeve of the service dress jacket or with battledress blouse immediately below the Corps or regimental titles worn at the top of the arm where the sleeve joins the shoulder-strap, and

---
* Army Council Instruction No. 872, Sept., 1948.   † War Office (A.G. 4)
‡ See page 161.

below group signs and parachute badges. When khaki drill jackets are worn with shoulder titles the formation badge is worn one inch below the top of the sleeve. The badges are not worn on greatcoats.

Some formations continue to wear the badges borne by the formations during the late war, and in the case of the 51st (Highland) Division (T.A.) the same as was worn during the 1914-18 War ; whilst others have incorporated portions of the war-time badges into new designs or on to new backgrounds—*e.g.*, Middle East Land Forces retained the camel of G.H.Q. M.E.F.; the 24th Engineer Group (T.A.) badge incorporates the old 55th (West Lancs) Division badge; the 44th (Home Counties) Division (T.A.) kept their red oval as a background to their new badge; and the 246th Scottish Beach Brigade† badge incorporated that of the 52nd (Lowland) Division.

The new badges which were introduced fell mainly into two categories: the Symbolic—*e.g.*, Aldershot District with its searchlights, reminiscent of the Aldershot Tattoo, and the torch of learning, symbolic of the many Training Establishments in the District; the knight's helmet and sword of the 56th (London) Armoured Division*; and the armoured Clydesdale of the 30th (Lowlands) Independent Armoured Brigade†; and the Heraldic—*e.g.*, the Irish harp of Northern Ireland District; the lion rampant of Scottish Command; the white horse of Hanover District, and the arms of York of Northern Command.

---

* This was the badge adopted when the Division was re-formed in 1947, but the badge was subsequently changed to one similar to that worn in the 1939-45 War—see page 95.
† This Brigade now (1952) wears the 52nd (Lowland) Division badge. See page 92.

The small letter "T" worn on shoulder straps or titles or below collar badges by the pre-war Territorial Army has not been reintroduced, but the adoption of distinctive badges for Territorial Army formations has the dual purpose of identifying the Territorial soldier, and creating an *esprit de corps* among the newly raised formations as well as maintaining that of the older ones. The importance attached to these badges of well-chosen, appropriate and distinctive designs has not been underestimated. They are now to be part of the dress of the soldier, who will be proud to be identified with the formation in which he serves.

As in war, the formation sign is put to further uses, in addition to being a cloth badge on the arm of the wearer. Firstly, as a vehicle marking, painted on the wings or tailboards of cars, trucks, A.F.Vs. and lorries. Secondly, as a directional sign and on notice boards. Thirdly, the signs are embroidered or sewn on the car pennants of senior officers—the red and black rectangular pennants of Army Commanders, the red swallow-tailed pennants of Divisional Commanders, the blue of Brigades and the green of Districts.

Lastly, the signs have been taken widely into use for die-stamped stationery, Christmas cards, routine orders, and other printed material used by formations.

The formation sign has its place in peace as much as it had in war, and as the years pass it takes on a wider significance by the development of its use.

POST - WAR FORMATION BADGES

THE WAR OFFICE

The War Office badge was first seen by the public on the 19th of August, 1946, when Field-Marshal Viscount Montgomery, then C.I.G.S., wore it on sailing for Canada. The design, introduced at Field-Marshal Montgomery's instigation, was the first distinguishing shoulder badge for the War Office Military Staff. Throughout the war years no distinguishing badge was worn by personnel employed at the War Office. When Staff Officers ceased to wear their armlets early in 1941, the War Office Staff ceased to wear any distinguishing sign—the official reason being that if such had been worn they might easily become a target for persons seeking information.

The badge is a golden shield, on it a smaller blue shield on which are three golden cannon; above the small shield are three cannon balls in blue. The badge is set on a background equally divided into red and dark blue, the colours of the War Office Staff Officer's armlet.

The badge is based on the arms of the Board of Ordnance,* no doubt on the grounds that the War Office assumed the functions of the Board of Ordnance on its abolition in 1855, together with the fact that the Army Council on its formation in 1904 adopted the same arms surmounting the Flags Union on the Army Council flags which were approved by King Edward VII in February, 1905.†

The Arms of the Board of Ordnance were adopted as the badge of the Army Ordnance Corps on its formation in 1896 when Queen Victoria, in July, gave her approval for the badges for the helmet, cap and collar "in accordance with the ancient arms of the Ordnance Department." Although it is known that the coat of arms of the Board of Ordnance was of ancient origin and was probably brought into use in Tudor times, the Board was not granted the right to bear the arms until the issue of a Royal Warrant dated 19th July, 1806.‡

---

* See page 216.
† This flag is flown over the War Office on official occasions.
‡ Royal Approval was given on the 6th July, 1806. The badge was registered at the College of Arms on the 16th May, 1823.

WAR OFFICE CONTROLLED UNITS

This badge was introduced in 1946 for all units, schools and training establishments directly under War Office control—*e.g.*, the Mons Officer Cadet School at Aldershot; the School of Artillery, Larkhill; the School of Military Engineering, etc. The badge has an evenly divided background, top half red, lower half dark blue, upon which is superimposed the Imperial Crown surmounted by a lion in yellow or gold.

MILITARY STAFF, MINISTRY OF SUPPLY

This badge, which is based on the crest of the coat of arms of the old Board of Ordnance,* depicts an arm and hand in pink, rising out of a yellow mural crown, the hand grasping a yellow winged thunderbolt from which spring four forks of lightning in white picked out in black. The design set on a blue circle. The heraldic description of this badge is: "In a circle azure out of a mural crown or, a dexter cubit arm proper, the hand grasping a thunderbolt argent winged or," symbolizing the arising, from defence, of the strong arm of Britain wielding modern weapons in the midst of endurance.

---

* See page 216.

SUPREME HEADQUARTERS
ALLIED POWERS EUROPE (SHAPE)

The badge of SHAPE (Supreme Headquarters Allied Powers Europe) was authorized on 5th October, 1951, for wear on the left sleeve. The badge consists of two unsheathed swords in gold, points uppermost, forming the letter "A" (for "Allied Powers"). The swords are superimposed on two sprays of olive leaves, also in gold, from which rise twelve silver rays, representative of the original signatories of the North Atlantic Treaty and symbolic of rays of hope. The design is enclosed in a golden scroll bearing in black letters the inscription VIGILIA PRETIUM LIBERTATIS ("Vigilance is the Price of Liberty"), which is the motif of the design, the olive leaves symbolizing the dedication of the North Atlantic Treaty Powers to peace, and the swords representative of the armed strength necessary to preserve that peace. The whole design is set on a green shield—the shield representing the nature of SHAPE's mission, the colour signifying the peaceful woods and fields of Europe—with the word SHAPE in silver set above the central design. This badge is worn by personnel of the British element of the Headquarters which is located in Paris.

H.Q. ALLIED LAND FORCES CENTRAL EUROPE
Commandement-en-chef des Forces, Terrestres Alliées Centre Europe.

No formation badge is worn by the personnel of this Headquarters at Fontainebleau which succeeded the Headquarters of the Western Europe Commanders-in-Chief [*] although a badge has appeared in print similar in design and colouring to that of the latter H.Q.; this badge has an additional gold link symbolizing the inclusion of the sixth Power—the United States of America—in the North Atlantic Treaty Powers who were signatories of the Brussels Treaty (Great Britain, France, Belgium, Holland and Luxembourg).

---

[*] See page 11.

H.Q. WESTERN EUROPE COMMANDERS-IN-CHIEF

This badge may well be regarded as the first truly international formation sign/badge, although the badge of S.H.A.E.F. (Supreme Headquarters Allied Expeditionary Force) was worn during the war (1944-46) by British, American and other allied officers, as were also the badges of A.F.H.Q. (Allied Force H.Q.) in North Africa and Italy, and S.A.C.S.E.A. (Supreme Allied Command South-East Asia) (the H.Q. Staff of Admiral Lord Louis Mountbatten). This badge was universally worn by the joint staff of the five Western Union Powers of the Brussels Treaty (Britain, France, Belgium, Holland and Luxembourg).

The badge, in which the five gold links forming a pentagon on a blue background symbolized the five Western Powers, was worn on the sleeve below the shoulder title in the same position as all British formation signs/badges. This badge was first seen (in Aldershot) in October, 1949, worn by Field-Marshal Viscount Montgomery when he visited the H.Q. of the Airborne Forces.

Home Commands

NORTHERN COMMAND

It was on the 1st of January, 1947, that the war-time badge of Northern Command—the green apple on a dark blue diamond*—was superseded by a red cross on a black shield; superimposed on the cross are five lions in gold (or yellow). York having been a military headquarters since earliest times, it was considered appropriate to adopt a badge linking Northern Command Headquarters with the local Civic Authority and traditions. The badge was therefore taken from the shield of the arms of the City of York, which is a red cross with the five lions (representing the five Saxon Generals who strenuously defended York against the Norman invaders) displayed thereon, set on a white shield, the colours of the Command sign having been taken to represent Command colours of red and black.

* The war-time badge was chosen at the time when the General Officer Commanding was General Sir Ronald F. Adam, Bt., G.C.B., D.S.O., O.B.E.; the badge depicting the green apple, on a blue diamond, being chosen to link with the name of the G.O.C.—viz., "Adam's Apple."

WESTERN COMMAND

The war-time badge of Western Command has been retained—the yellow cross of St. David of Wales with the red rose of Lancaster in the centre within a red circle on a black background.

EASTERN COMMAND

The war-time Eastern Command badge, the white bulldog on the black background, was replaced in 1947 by a shield on which is a design incorporating portions of the signs of the Districts composing the Command. The white cliffs of the South-East Coast (Home Counties District),* the crossed swords from the badge of the former East Central District, and the Viking's head of East Anglian District.* The colouring of the shield is made up of blue sea, white cliffs, green downs, blue sky, swords with white blades and red hilts, and the Viking's head in red and white.

---

* See page 36.

SOUTHERN COMMAND

Southern Command has retained its war-time badge, the conventional representation of the stars of the Southern Cross set on a shield, the colouring of the shield and the stars varying according to the arm of the service of the unit of the wearer. There are eighteen variations of the colouring of the Command badge. That of Command Headquarters is a red shield with a central black horizontal band and the five stars in white. In all cases the badges worn by personnel contain five stars—three in a row in the centre, with one above and one below the central star—but when used as a vehicle marking there are six stars, the additional star being placed immediately below the lower star. The vehicle marking background is rectangular, the shield being confined to the arm badges.

SCOTTISH COMMAND

Scottish Command has retained the sign it adopted during the war. The heraldic lion rampant of Scotland in gold on a background evenly divided horizontally into two red and a central black band.

ANTI-AIRCRAFT COMMAND

The famous war-time badge of Anti-Aircraft Command has been retained by the Headquarters and all Groups,

Brigades, and units of A.A. Command, with a few exceptions. The exceptions are Heavy and Light Anti-Aircraft Regiments, which until recently formed part of Anti-Aircraft A.G.R.As. Most of these units continue to wear the formation badges approved for the A.G.R.As., although they now form part of A.A. Brigades of A.A. Command.*

The badge is the well-known black bow and arrow aimed upwards, set on a scarlet square. Originally this badge was worn only by the Headquarters Staff of A.A. Command, but in 1943 it was universally adopted for all formations and units of A.D.G.B. (Air Defence of Great Britain). The badge is symbolic of defence against air attack, but its choice was influenced by the crest of the Gordon family,† of which the badge is a reproduction, which by coincidence appeared above the entrance of "Glenthorne" at Stanmore, the house (which was built by a member of the Gordon family in the late nineteenth century) taken over in 1939 as the Command Headquarters; also the fact that the badge of the pre-war School of Anti-Aircraft Defence at Biggin Hill was a kneeling nude archer, his bow and arrow pointing skywards.

---

* See pages 106-109.
† During the 1914-18 War a badge of similar design but with different colouring (grey and white) was the sign of 9th Corps and was adopted by the Corps Commander, Lieut.-General Sir Alexander Hamilton-Gordon.

Overseas Commands

G.H.Q. MIDDLE EAST LAND FORCES (M.E.L.F.)

It was in the latter part of 1947 that G.H.Q. Middle East Land Forces, in the Canal Zone of Egypt, adopted as its badge a yellow camel set on a shield evenly divided into Army colours of red (top) and blue (lower half). During the 1939-45 War personnel of G.H.Q. Middle East Forces did not wear any distinguishing badge, although the G.H.Q. badge which was used as a vehicle marking was a brown or golden camel set on a black square background. The camel design was retained when G.H.Q. M.E.F. became G.H.Q. M.E.L.F. in 1946 and incorporated into the new formation badge when it was generally adopted in the following year.

G.H.Q. FAR EAST LAND FORCES (FARELF)

The war-time badge of A.L.F.S.E.A. (Allied Land Forces South East Asia) continued to be worn by H.Q. South East Asia Land Forces (S.E.A.L.F.) when that formation succeeded A.L.F.S.E.A. in December, 1946. On the 15th of August, 1947, the designation was changed to G.H.Q. Far East Land Forces, but the old A.L.F.S.E.A. badge was retained. The badge is composed of a white shield; on it a red Crusader's cross. Behind the shield, the wings of Victory in yellow (or gold) and a Crusader's sword in white; the whole set on a background of light blue with a dark blue base. The badge is emblematic of the wings of Victory carrying the Crusader's sword and shield across the seas to the liberation of the enemy-occupied territories and to the defeat of Japan, and symbolizing the combined efforts of all three Services in that theatre of operations.

H.Q. BRITISH TROOPS IN EGYPT AND MEDITERRANEAN COMMAND

The British lion, guardant and crowned in yellow, set on a square divided horizontally, two portions, equal sized, being red and black—Army colours—and a lower, narrower band of light blue, symbolic of the Mediterranean, is the appropriate distinguishing badge of the Headquarters of British Troops in Egypt (B.T.E.) and Mediterranean Command.

MALAYA COMMAND

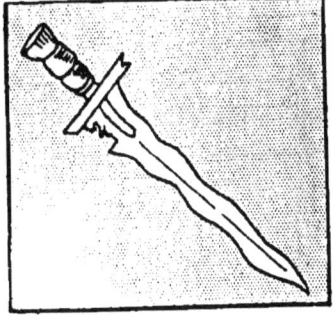

This Command, established after the liberation of Malaya in 1945, adopted as its badge a kris, the native Malayan dagger with a wavy shaped blade, in yellow picked out in black, set on a green background.

EAST AFRICA COMMAND

The East Africa Command badge is a scarlet circle, surrounded by a black ring set on a khaki square. Within the circle a pair of pangas, crossed left over right, each with silver blades and black handles. When used on vehicles the badge is eight inches in diameter, the black border half an inch in width and the pangas six and a half inches long. This is similar to the war-time badge of the Command, which was crossed pangas on a bright green background.

WEST AFRICA COMMAND

A golden palm tree on a two-inch-square red background with a black horizontal bar is the badge worn by all troops of West Africa Command in Nigeria, Sierre Leone, Gambia and the Gold Coast. The badge is adapted from that of the Royal West African Frontier Force, which is a yellow palm tree set above a scroll bearing the letters "R.W.A.F.F." on a green circle. This Command has also adopted a series

of badges (all incorporating the palm tree emblem) for the three Districts of the Command.*

H.Q. LAND FORCES HONG KONG

Established on the liberation of Hong Kong in 1945, this H.Q. has adopted as its badge that which was in use by H.Q. China Command prior to the 1939-45 War—a China dragon in gold set on a rectangular background of Command colours, red, black and red.

* See page 49.

BRITISH COMMONWEALTH FORCES, KOREA

British Commonwealth Forces, Korea, wear the badge which was introduced in 1946 for wear by the British Commonwealth occupation Forces in Japan. (Then composed of the 5th British Infantry Brigade, the 268th Indian Brigade and the 34th Australian Infantry Brigade and the 9th New Zealand Brigade.) The badge is composed of the Imperial Crown in gold and red set above a dark blue scroll outlined in red on which is an inscription in white, "British Commonwealth Forces." The design is set on a square dark blue background and is worn today by British Commonwealth Forces in Japan and Korea, other than by those entitled to wear the badge of the First Commonwealth Division.

BRITISH TROOPS IN PALESTINE

The badge worn by British Troops in Palestine, up to the end of the British Mandate in Palestine, other than those wearing their own Divisional or other formation badge, was an Arab knife, a white blade and black hilt, set on a red square.

BRITISH ELEMENT TRIESTE FORCE
(BETFOR)

This force continues to wear the war-time badge of the 13th Corps—a leaping red gazelle in a white circle on a red diamond with a narrow white border—the badge which was adopted by the Corps in the Western Desert. The Corps fought across Africa and in Italy and at the cessation of hostilities in 1945 occupied Austria and the north-eastern portion of Italy, including Trieste, where in the year following the war it became, on the disbandment of the Corps, the Headquarters of the British Element of the Trieste Force.

BRITISH TROOPS IN FRANCE

After the cessation of hostilities, there were still a number of British troops in France in the former "Rear Maintenance Area" in the Normandy Beach-head and at several Base depots, transit camps and with other administrative Headquarters. The numbers of troops rapidly decreased, but the maintenance of certain installations continued, together with the administrative Headquarters of R.E. Movement Control Units, Graves Registration Detachments, etc. The troops wore as their distinguishing sign the original badge of G.H.Q. Troops, 21st Army Group—a blue cross on a red shield.

BRITISH TROOPS IN AUSTRIA

The original occupational force in Austria was made up of Eighth Army units, and British troops in Austria, after the disbandment of the Eighth Army, subsequently adopted as their distinguishing sign the former Eighth Army badge—the Crusader's cross in gold on a white shield with a gold border set on a dark blue background.

British Army of the Rhine

H.Q. BRITISH ARMY OF THE RHINE

When H.Q. 21st Army Group* was, in August, 1945, redesignated H.Q. British Army of the Rhine, the H.Q. 21st Army Group badge, two Crusaders' swords in gold, set on a dark blue cross on a red shield, was retained by H.Q. B.A.O.R.

RHINE ARMY TROOPS

This badge was adopted on 21st April, 1947, for use by all troops in the British Army of the Rhine other than those of H.Q. B.A.O.R.: 1 British Corps District, Hamburg District; all Divisions and Brigades on the B.A.O.R. Order of Battle (in possession of their own formation badge); British Troops, Berlin; British Troops in the Low Countries; the B.A.O.R.

---

* 21st Army Group was formed in 1943 and, composed of Second Army and 1st Canadian Army, carried out the invasion of North-West Europe in June, 1944, fighting its way from the Normandy beaches to the Baltic to the final defeat of the German Armies in May, 1945.

Training Centre; the B.A.O.R. R.A.C. and Engineer Training Centres; The School of Artillery and Air Formation Signals. The Rhine Army Troops' badge is an adaptation of the H.Q. B.A.O.R. (former H.Q. 21st Army Group) badge, and was composed of a Crusader's sword in yellow set on a red cross, superimposed on a dark blue shield (the reversed colours of the former G.H.Q. Troops, 21st Army Group badge).

BRITISH TROOPS, BERLIN

Adopted shortly after the occupation of Berlin in 1945, the distinguishing badge of the troops in the British sector of Berlin was a plain black circle surrounded by a scarlet ring. In 1952 this badge was changed slightly by the addition of a black top on which, in red, is the word "Berlin."

SCHOOL OF ARTILLERY, B.A.O.R.

The former badge of 21st Army Group G.H.Q. Troops, a red shield with a dark blue Crusader's cross, has been adopted by the School of Artillery, B.A.O.R., with a field gun in gold—of the same design as that of the R.A. cap-badge and buttons—set on the lower portion of the vertical of the blue cross, and the letters "S of A" in gold set on the horizontal of the cross.

ENGINEER TRAINING ESTABLISHMENT, B.A.O.R.

The R.E. collar-badge (the grenade above a scroll upon which is the Corps motto "Ubique") in yellow set in the centre of the red shield, with blue Crusader's cross, the former badge of the G.H.Q. Troops, 21st Army Group, was the badge of the Engineer Centre Establishment at Hameln (Hamelin) in Germany.

R.A.C. TRAINING CENTRE, B.A.O.R.

A tank, in white, similar to that in the badge of the Royal Tank Regiment, set in the centre of crossed lances, also in white, emblematic of the cavalry regiments now incorporated in the Royal Armoured Corps, the design superimposed on the blue Crusader's cross on the red shield badge of the 21st Army Group G.H.Q. and L. of C. troops, is the badge adopted by the Royal Armoured Corps Training Centre of the Rhine Army.

RHINE ARMY TRAINING CENTRE

The Rhine Army All Arms Training Centre, located at Sennelager, near Paderborn, adopted as its badge the badge of 21st Army Group G.H.Q. troops, with the addition of the torch of learning as used as a road sign in U.K. to denote a school, in yellow, set on the vertical of the blue Crusader's cross.

CONTROL COMMISSION, GERMANY (C.C.G.)

The Control Commission for Germany adopted, soon after the cessation of hostilities, the familiar badge of G.H.Q. Troops, 21st Army Group, the blue cross on the red shield, with the addition of the letters "CCG" linked, in yellow, superimposed in the centre of the blue cross. The badge, set in the top left-hand corner of a dark blue flag, is flown from the C.C.G. Headquarter offices throughout the British zone.

HANOVER DISTRICT (B.A.O.R.)

Hanover District of the British Army of the Rhine adopted in 1948 as its badge a representation of the white horse of Hanover set on a red shield.

HAMBURG DISTRICT (B.A.O.R.)

Hamburg District inherited the former badge of H.Q. L. of C., 21st Army Group, which, after the war, was also worn by H.Q. British Troops in the Low Countries. The well-known badge is a dark blue cross on a yellow shield.

RHINE DISTRICT (B.A.O.R.)

This District of Rhine Army has adopted the same formation badge as worn by Hamburg District—a dark blue cross and a yellow shield.

AQUATIC TRAINING SCHOOL (B.A.O.R.)

Located on the shores of Kiel Bay on the Baltic, this training establishment adopted the appropriate sign of a white duck on a circle divided to represent sky and sea, the colours being light and dark blue. At this establishment men are trained in light bridging, watermanship, rafting and boating, and are taught to swim.

Home Districts and Garrisons

LONDON DISTRICT

Adopted during the war, London District has retained the badge of the mural crown in gold, with a sword in red pointing upwards through the centre. The design is in a dark blue rectangle cut at the corners, the sword having been taken from the arms of the City of London and the mural crown from the crest of the London County Council.

NORTHERN IRELAND DISTRICT

The familiar white gate on the light green background which was the badge of Northern Ireland District until 1948 has been superseded by a new badge, a dark green shield with a narrow yellow border; on the centre of the shield is a crowned Irish harp—of the same design as the cap-badge of the Royal Ulster Rifles—in yellow, picked out in black.

HIGHLAND DISTRICT
SCOTTISH COMMAND

Highland District has retained the war-time badge of North Highland District. This, following the style set by H.Q. Scottish Command (and adopted also by Lowland District and 105th Coast Brigade, R.A. (T.A.)), is the heraldic Scottish lion rampant in gold set on a square background divided diagonally, the lower portion being dark purple, the upper dark green—the Highland Brigade colours—symbolic of the heather and moorlands of the Scottish Highlands.

LOWLAND DISTRICT
SCOTTISH COMMAND

This District, with its Headquarters in Glasgow, has replaced the war-time West Scotland District, and continues to wear the badge of that District: the heraldic Scottish lion rampant in yellow superimposed upon a white St. Andrew's cross on a red square.

ALDERSHOT DISTRICT

SOUTHERN COMMAND

This badge was adopted by Headquarters, Aldershot District, in July, 1948, and is worn by the H.Q. Staff and all units directly under command of that Headquarters. It was designed by the then G.O.C., the late Major-General J. A. Baillon, C.B., C.B.E., M.C. The badge is a shield, the base of which is green and the upper portion blue—the blue of a summer night sky. Across the sky are two white searchlight beams which are significant of the pre-war Aldershot Tattoo which was so closely associated with the pre-war Aldershot Command in the minds of a very wide section of the population. Superimposed on this background is a yellow torch of learning, significant of the fact that the majority of military units now stationed in Aldershot are Training Establishments and Schools of Instruction.

The introduction of this badge saw the passing of the badge which had been worn by troops in Aldershot since 1944—namely, the white winged figure of Victory set on a saxe-blue background representing sea and sky, and before her the white points of The Needles.

This was originally the badge of Hants and Dorset District of Southern Command, and it was introduced in 1943. The district was subsequently redesignated Aldershot and Hants District, and in 1947 the designation was changed again and it became known as Aldershot District. The wartime badge which had been inherited from the original Hants and Dorset District therefore lost much of its significance. This badge is more appropriately associated with Aldershot District, its past activities and its role today.

SOUTH-WESTERN DISTRICT
SOUTHERN COMMAND

The war-time badge—the black francolin partridge on a white oval—is still worn by this District, which covers South-West England. South-Western District assumed its

SOUTH-WESTERN DISTRICT
(see page 34)

A new badge for South-Western District was introduced in July, 1953, to replace that described on page 34. The new badge depicts a hind trippant and is a facsimile of the actual crest on Sir Francis Drake's ship the *Golden Hind*. It was the arms of Sir Christopher Hatton, a courtier of Queen Elizabeth's who joined Drake's ship the *Pelican* as Captain of the Queen's Bodyguard. He acquitted himself so well that the ship's name was changed to the *Golden Hind*, and although the pelican still remained as a figure-head on the bows, Sir Christopher's crest was mounted on the quarter-deck.

This badge was adopted by South-Western District as the District covers the large south-western seaboard area. The golden hind is set on a green square as this background colour is appropriate to a district headquarters and was adopted for this reason instead of the blue background generally associated with the sea.

title in 1943 when it replaced the 8th Corps District, the Corps being relieved of its static commitments to train in its operational role for service with 21st Army Group in North-West Europe. The District badge was adopted in the early days of the war when the 8th Corps was commanded by General Sir Harold E. Franklyn, K.C.B., D.S.O., M.C., the francolin partridge being chosen as an association with the name of the Corps Commander.

SALISBURY PLAIN DISTRICT
SOUTHERN COMMAND

This District has retained its war-time badge—which was adopted in 1941—for it would undoubtedly be difficult to find a more appropriate sign. The badge depicts the Great Cromlech of Stonehenge in red, with, in the rear, other stones of the Druids' circle in black. This is set on a yellow background with a grass-green base within a red circle. The badge was designed in the spring of 1944 by Captain Walter Clark, F.R.I.B.A., R.E., then serving on the staff of the District H.Q. The design of the Cromlech is correct in outline and proportion. The dominating colour, red, was chosen for its striking qualities.

HOME COUNTIES DISTRICT
EASTERN COMMAND

This District has retained the war-time badge of East Kent District—a shield on which is depicted Dover Castle in black set on green downs above the white cliffs and the sea. This sign is also incorporated into the sign of the 44th (Home Counties) Division (T.A.).

EAST ANGLIAN DISTRICT
EASTERN COMMAND

This badge* was adopted by East Anglian District in October, 1946. It was designed by Lieut.-Colonel W. S. Shepherd, former O.C. No. 15 Infantry Training Centre at Colchester, and was composed of a Viking's head in white set on a red shield. The design was chosen to link the association of the Vikings with East Anglia, which was included in the Danelaw after the defeat of the Viking Guthrum in A.D. 878 by Alfred, King of Wessex.

---
* See also page 73.

NORTH-WESTERN DISTRICT
WESTERN COMMAND

The red rose of Lancaster set on a dark green background within a yellow entwined circular border is the present badge of this District, which was formed in 1944 by the redesignation of the Lancs and Border District with the incorporation of part of West Lancs District. The present North-Western District badge was the badge of the former Lancs and Border District.

MID-WESTERN DISTRICT
WESTERN COMMAND

The Prince of Wales's feathers, in red, on a dark green circle constitutes the badge of this District of Western Command. This was the badge of the war-time North Wales District which when raised, with its Headquarters at Shrewsbury, comprised the six North Wales counties—Anglesey, Caernarvon, Denbigh, Flint, Montgomery, and

Merioneth—and the border county of Shropshire. The District was redesignated Midland West District in 1944 when part of the former West Lancashire District was absorbed into its boundaries.

NORTHUMBRIAN DISTRICT
NORTHERN COMMAND

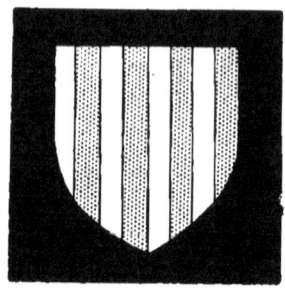

The badge of Northumbrian District, which has its Headquarters at Catterick Camp, is St. Oswald's Shield composed of eight yellow and red vertical bars set on a shield which is on a square blue background. St. Oswald was the first Christian King of Northumbria in the seventh century, who, it is said, used to come out of battle with his golden shield streaked with blood. The District Badge was taken from the badge used by the Northumbrian County Council. The badge, with three red and three yellow bars, was adopted during the late war by the Northumbrian Battalions of the Home Guard and when Northumbrian District came into existence in 1942 this badge was adopted, the design being changed in 1946.

NORTH-MIDLAND DISTRICT
NORTHERN COMMAND

This District has retained its war-time badge; a figure, set on a grass-green square, depicting Robin Hood clad in Lincoln green, with brown cap, feather, gloves, belt, quiver and boots, with long-bow and arrow in black. This badge is appropriate inasmuch as Sherwood Forest is within the District's boundaries, and the District Headquarters are near Nottingham.

EAST AND WEST RIDINGS AREA
NORTHERN COMMAND

This Area of Northern Command has adopted the white rose of Yorkshire set on a black square.

CATTERICK GARRISON
NORTHERN COMMAND

This Garrison was permitted to retain the Catterick District badge when that District was re-absorbed in 1952 into Northumbrian District (which has its H.Q. at Catterick Camp). Catterick District during the war years (1939-45) formed part of Northumbrian, and later North Riding, District, and did not possess a badge of its own until it was re-established as a District in 1947 when it adopted the Tudor Rose in red and white set on a dark green square. The design depicts the white and red roses of York and Lancaster and is taken from the Arms of Richmond, Yorks, in view of that town's proximity and close associations with Catterick. The combination of the red and white roses commemorates the union of the houses of York and Lancaster by the marriage of Elizabeth of York with the Earl of Richmond, afterwards King Henry VII.

SOLENT GARRISON

Two golden keys, representing the keys of the King's Gate and the Landport Gate to the City of Portsmouth, set on a rectangle evenly divided, top half red, lower half purple.

In Stuart times, Portsmouth became a Royal fortress with a governor appointed by the King. Like many of its kind it was walled and moated, and had many gates, but the walls disappeared later and the moat was filled in. However, two of the gates remain to this day, although they are not on their original sites. These gates are the King's or King James's Gate, and the Town or Landport Gate, and they stand at the entrances of the United Service Recreation ground, officers' and men's entrances respectively. The gold keys actually turn the locks of these gates, but ordinary base metal keys have been made for general use. The key with the Royal crown at the top is that of the King's Gate, and the key with the star and crescent of the arms of the City of Portsmouth fits the Landport Gate. Now that there is no longer a governor appointed by the

King, the keys are held by the Garrison Commander as the senior military officer and not by the Naval Commander-in-Chief.

By a custom which seems to have started in George III's time the keys were always brought by the Military Commander and offered to the reigning Sovereign on a visit to Portsmouth. The custom was carried on in the time of Queen Victoria but seems to have lapsed for some years. It was revived in 1947 and the keys were offered to H.M. King George on his visit to South Africa. The keys are carried on a crimson cushion with gold tassels and tied together with a crimson and purple ribbon bearing the Royal Arms.

SHOEBURYNESS GARRISON
(MINISTRY OF SUPPLY EXPERIMENTAL ESTABLISHMENT, SHOEBURYNESS)

The badge of Shoeburyness Garrison was an old-time cannon in yellow on a cobalt blue oblong background. When the Garrison, as an administrative formation, ceased to exist, the badge was retained by all personnel of the Ministry of Supply Experimental Establishment at Shoeburyness.

Overseas Areas, Districts and Garrisons

1st INFANTRY DIVISION DISTRICT, M.E.L.F.

This District has adopted a sign based on the sign of the 1st Division—a plain white equilateral triangle and incorporating the badge of the former Tripolitania District.

The District sign is a white equilateral triangle, in the centre of which is the black Barbary pirate's galley with three white sails on a blue wavy sea—the design taken from the emblem of the city of Tripoli. Below the triangle is a white scroll, the turned-in ends in red; on the scroll the motto of the 1st Division—"Primus Inter Pares" ("First Among Equals"). On either side of the triangle are white scrolls, protruding from each a yellow ear of corn.

TRIPOLITANIA DISTRICT, M.E.L.F.

This badge, the emblem of the City of Tripoli, which stands on a pillar outside the *Castello* on the ceremonial jetty at Tripoli, was adapted from the war-time formation sign of the District, and is a Barbary pirate's galley in black, set against a white background, on a blue sea within a shield with a black border.

CYRENAICA DISTRICT, M.E.L.F.

The war-time distinctive sign of this District, which was designed by the first District Commander, Major-General A. L. Collier, C.B.E., M.C., when the Headquarters was established in 1943,* was two Greek pillars (in black) on black paving stones set on a white square, significant of the "parts of Libya about Cyrene" (*Acts., ch.* 2, *verse* 10). Cyrene, where there still remain some magnificent Greek and Roman remains, was one of the most flourishing Greek colonies and was later of considerable importance during the Roman occupation. The existing badge bears the same design, but now the pillars and pavings are white, picked out in black on a black square.

ERITREA DISTRICT

Eritrea, the former Italian colony which saw much heavy fighting in 1940-41 and was occupied by British troops for eleven years, became federated with Abyssinia in September, 1952, and British responsibility for Administration and law and order ceased. The last British Battalion to leave Eritrea

---

* The H.Q. was established in Benghazi in February, 1943, moving to Barce the following month.

was the 1st Bn. The South Wales Borderers, who beat
"Retreat" before the lowering of the Union Jack at Asmara
on the 15th September, 1952.

The badge of Eritrea District was not worn on uniform,
but was used in other forms. It took the form of the Lion of
Ethiopia in gold set above twelve wavy green lines, set on a
shield in gold outline.

CYPRUS DISTRICT, M.E.L.F.

Two lions passant guardant in gold set on a green shield
is the badge of Cyprus District, M.E.L.F. This badge is
adapted from the Arms of Cyprus which are based on
those of the Lucignian Kings of Cyprus (*circa* 1192-1489).

CANAL SOUTH DISTRICT, M.E.L.F.

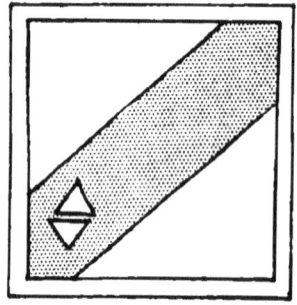

Similar to the war-time badge of No. 18 (Suez Canal) Area M.E.F., the badge of Canal South District which was, until 1952, designated the 17th Infantry Brigade District of Middle East Land Forces is appropriately one depicting the Suez Canal, a diagonal light blue band, on it in the lower left-hand corner two small white triangles representing a felucca, the blue band set on a yellow square representing the desert, with a narrow pale green border symbolic of the delta.

CANAL NORTH DISTRICT, M.E.L.F.

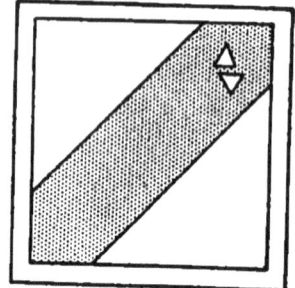

Identical in design with the badge of Canal South District, M.E.L.F., except that the felucca is set at the top right-hand corner of the blue band symbolizing the canal, this badge was adopted on the reorganization in 1952 of the Canal Zone Districts.

CARIBBEAN AREA

The war-time badge of North Caribbean Area was a black sea-horse picked out in yellow set on a khaki rectangle set above a red bar, whilst that of South Caribbean Area was crossed swords in black on a yellow background. The present badge of the Caribbean Area is a black sea-horse on a yellow rectangle. This badge was worn by the 2nd Bn. The Gloucestershire Regiment, who were serving in Jamaica at the time of the threat to British Honduras in February, 1948, and served in the Colony—the first British regiment ever to set foot in that country—to protect it from possible invasion from Guatemala.

It is now worn by all troops stationed in the British West Indies—Jamaica, Antigua, St. Lucia, Barbados, Grenada, Trinidad and Tobago—and in British Guiana and British Honduras.

SINGAPORE DISTRICT

This District was formed in February, 1946, under the command of Major-General L. H. Cox, C.B., C.B.E., M.C., with its Headquarters in Singapore, and took over the administration of the former No. 2 Area, S.E.A.C. The District boundaries remained the same as those of No. 2 Area until the end of November, 1947, when the British troops withdrew from the Netherlands East Indies and the Riow Archipelago was handed back to the Dutch authorities. The District badge, adapted from the Colony crest, is composed of a lion and a palm tree in yellow on a dark green background.

THE WEST AFRICAN DISTRICTS

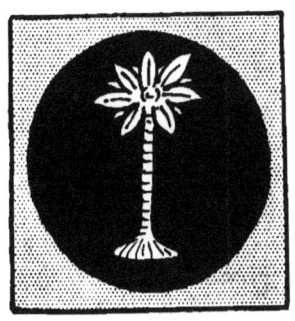

GOLD COAST DISTRICT

A palm tree in gold on a black circle on a two-inch yellow square.

NIGERIA DISTRICT

A golden palm tree on a black circle set on a green square.

SIERRA LEONE AND GAMBIA DISTRICT

A palm tree in gold set on a black circle on a square blue background.

MALTA GARRISON

Malta Garrison has retained the war-time badge of Malta Command—a scarlet shield, with a central black band in the centre of which is a white Maltese cross.

GIBRALTAR GARRISON

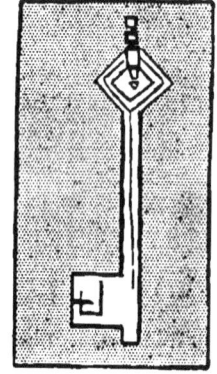

A yellow key picked out in black set on a scarlet rectangle is the appropriate badge worn by the Fortress Headquarters Staff and the Garrison of Gibraltar other than Royal Artillery units, who wear the key on a background of Regimental Colours—"The Key to the Mediterranean." The key is taken from the coat of arms of the Rock.

CEYLON GARRISON

The badge of Ceylon Garrison was an elephant's head in yellow set on a blue background. This was an adaptation of the former Ceylon Army Command sign, which was of the same design but with a background of Command colours—red, black and red.

GAZA SUB-DISTRICT

This Administrative District of British Forces in Palestine, 1947-48, adopted as its badge a black silhouetted figure representing Samson, holding in outstretched arms two white pillars (of the Temple) set on a red square. The badge, which although adopted was never issued for wear by the troops in the District owing to the end of the British Mandate before manufacture, was symbolic of the times, Samson's destruction of the Temple being analogical with the state of affairs in Palestine during the latter days of the British Mandate.

F

Regular Army Formations

1ST CORPS

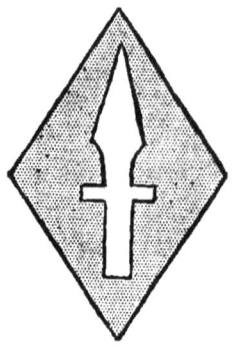

Re-formed in Rhine Army in 1951, 1st Corps has retained the white spearhead on a scarlet diamond badge worn by the Corps in the 1939-45 War. The badge was then chosen to symbolize the operational role of the formation —the spearhead of the B.E.F. as it was in 1939-40—and again it was the spearhead of the British assaulting force in the D Day landings in Normandy on 6th June, 1944.

6TH ARMOURED DIVISION

The appropriate wartime badge of this formation, a clenched mailed fist in white on a black square, was readopted by this Division when re-formed in 1950.*

---

* During the late war the Division first saw active service with the First Army in Tunisia. It afterwards served in the campaign in Italy with the Eighth Army.

7TH ARMOURED DIVISION

The 7th Armoured Division, with the British Army of the Rhine, continues to wear the war-time badge of the formation: a brown desert rat picked out in white, set on a black rectangle. The Division was the first formation to go into action in the Western Desert in 1940, and it was in the sands and barren wastes of Libya that it earned its title of "The Desert Rats" because of its "scurrying and biting" tactics, likened to those of the jerboa (the desert rat).*

11TH ARMOURED DIVISION

Re-formed in 1950, this Armoured formation has retained the badge it bore in the late war†: a charging black bull with red horns, eyes and hooves, on a yellow oblong background.

---

* The Division served in the Western Desert from 1940 until the defeat of the Axis forces in 1943, following which the Division was withdrawn to serve in North-West Europe with 21st Army Group.

† During the late war this formation served with 21st Army Group in North-West Europe.

1st INFANTRY DIVISION

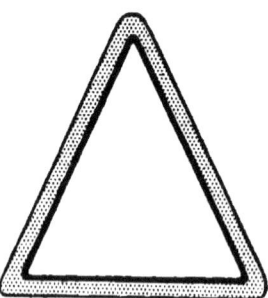

The simple war-time white triangle badge of the formation has been retained by this Regular Army Division, the symbolism of the badge being derived from the fact that the badge of the 1st Corps was (and still is*) a white spearhead—the spearhead of the B.E.F.—on a red diamond. The 1st Regular Division formed part of this Corps and took the tip of the spearhead as its sign.†

The present badge, one of the smallest formation badges, is an equilateral triangle, each side 1¼ in. When worn by the Divisional Staff and the Infantry it has a narrow scarlet border, and by units of the Royal Armoured Corps with a narrow yellow border.

---

* See page 52.
† During the 1939-45 War the 1st Division saw service with the B.E.F., 1939-40, in North Africa with First Army in 1942-43, and in Italy until the cessation of hostilities.

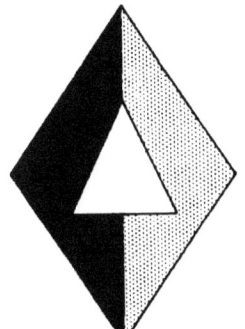

The Royal Artillery of the 1st Division wear a distinguishing badge with a small white equilateral triangle, each side 1 in., set in the centre of a diamond, with 2 in. sides. The diamond divided vertically into equal portions of dark blue and red, the Royal Artillery colours.

The Royal Signals of the Division wear a similar badge, with the small white triangle, set in the upper portion of the diamond which is dark blue, thereby combining the Royal Signals colours—blue and white.

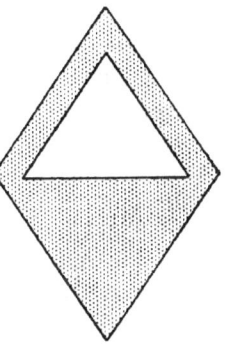

The Royal Army Service Corps units of the 1st Division wear a badge identical in design with that worn by the Royal Artillery, the diamond being evenly divided vertically into the R.A.S.C. colours of dark blue and yellow.

2ND INFANTRY DIVISION

This Regular Army formation, part of the British Army of the Rhine, continues to wear its war-time formation badge; two white keys, crossed, on a black square. The badge was derived from the coat of arms of the Archbishop of York, which contained the crossed keys, for in the earliest days in the history of British arms, when it was the practice, in time of need, to raise two armies, one from the North and one from the South, this device was borne on the shields and banners of the second or Northern Army, raised in those days by the Archbishop of York.*

---

* Between 1939 and 1945 the 2nd Division served with the B.E.F., 1939-40, in India from 1942 to 1944, and then in Burma with the Fourteenth Army until the end of the war.

3RD INFANTRY DIVISION

This Regular Division, re-formed in 1951, has retained the badge worn by the Division in the late war, a red triangle surrounded by three black triangles of equal size, the whole forming an equilateral triangle.*

---

* The 3rd Division formed part of the B.E.F., 1939-40, and was the Assault Division of 21st Army Group in the Normandy landing in June, 1944, serving in North-West Europe until the final defeat of the German Armies.

40TH DIVISION

The present badge of this formation is a yellow cock with red comb, beak and legs, set on a royal blue square. It has a link with the sign worn by the 40th Division in the 1914-18 War, when the formation wore a bantam cock on a white diamond. This Divisional sign was originally a plain diamond, but as this was similar to that worn by the 48th (South Midland) Division it was decided, in 1917, to add a bantam cock in the centre of the diamond, for the 40th were originally a "Bantam" Division, *i.e.*, composed of personnel of below normal height. The 40th Division was re-formed in Hong Kong in 1949, and it was from this formation that the 1st Bn. The Middlesex Regiment, 1st Bn. The Argyll and Sutherland Highlanders, and supporting troops were drawn to form the 27th British Commonwealth Brigade* for service in the operations in Korea in August-October, 1950.

---

* See page 67.

FIRST COMMONWEALTH DIVISION

First Style Badge

Raised in Korea in July, 1951, under the command of Major-General A. J. H. Cassels, and composed of the 28th and 29th Infantry Brigades,* with Australian, New Zealand and Indian units,† and the 25th Canadian Infantry Brigade. This first formation to be made up of Commonwealth troops adopted as its badge the Imperial Crown in gold, on a white background, above the word "Commonwealth" in gold on a white panel set on an azure blue shield.‡

The badge was later changed. The white backing to the crown was deleted, and the cap of maintenance in red was added and the white panel on which was set the word "Commonwealth" in gold was also removed.

* See page 67.
† 3rd Bn. Royal Australian Regiment, 16th Field Regiment, Royal New Zealand Artillery, and 60th Indian Field Ambulance.
‡ Similar to the colours of the ribbon of the campaign medal authorized in July, 1951, for service in Korea with the United Nations Forces.

The Division was formed on the 28th of July, 1951, at a short ceremony held at noon on that day, which was attended by the Commander of the 8th U.S. Army, and the Commander-in-Chief, British Commonwealth Forces in Japan. Major-General Cassels, then G.O.C. of the Division, unfurled the Divisional Flag, to fly alongside those of the United Kingdom, Canada, Australia, New Zealand, India and the United Nations, and the first completely Commonwealth Division came into existence symbolizing the determination and unity of the Commonwealth to play its part in the struggle against Communist aggression. At the time of its formation the Division was composed of:

25th Canadian Infantry Brigade, made up of the 2nd Bn. Princess Patricia's Canadian Light Infantry, the 2nd Bn. The Royal Canadian Regiment, and the 2nd Bn. The Royal 22ᵉ Regiment.

28th British Commonwealth Infantry Brigade, composed of the 1st Bn. The King's Own Scottish Borderers, 1st Bn. The King's Shropshire Light Infantry, and the 3rd Bn. Royal Australian Regiment.

29th British Infantry Brigade, comprising the 1st Bn. The Royal Northumberland Fusiliers, 1st Bn. The Gloucestershire Regiment, and 1st Bn. The Royal Ulster Rifles.

The 8th King's Royal Irish Hussars and a squadron of Lord Strathcona's Horse composed the Divisional Armour, together with British and New Zealand Artillery, British Sappers and British and Indian Field Ambulances.

Since the formation of the Division, now commanded by

Major-General M. M. Alston-Roberts-West, C.B., D.S.O., the 8th Hussars have been relieved by the 5th Royal Inniskilling Dragoon Guards, who in turn have been relieved by the 1st Royal Tank Regiment, and the following infantry battalions have also served, or are now serving, with the Division: 1st Bn. The Royal Norfolk Regiment, 1st Bn. The Welch Regiment, 1st Bn. The Royal Leicestershire Regiment, 1st Bn. The Black Watch, 1st Bn. The Royal Fusiliers, 1st Bn. The Durham Light Infantry, 1st Bn. The Duke of Wellington's Regiment, and the 1st Bn. The King's Regiment.*

Second Style Badge

---

* The 1st Bn. The Middlesex Regiment, and the 1st Bn. The Argyll and Sutherland Highlanders have also served in Korea. They were the first Battalions to land in the theatre of operations in 1950, and formed part of the 27th Infantry Brigade (see page 67) before the formation of the Commonwealth Division.

17TH GURKHA DIVISION

The 17th Gurkha Division, which now forms part of the British Army in the Far East, grew from the Gurkha Brigade and wears a badge of the same design as the wartime 43rd Lorried Infantry Brigade, which was crossed kukris in white on a dark green background. The background is now dark blue. The kukris in white are either woven on to this background, or are in white metal, and fastened to the blue patch by pins through the cloth.

25TH ARMOURED BRIGADE

This Armoured Brigade has adopted as its badge a rhinoceros on a white oval on a black rectangle. Similar in style to that worn by the 1st Armoured Division in the late war and symbolic of armoured force.

Infantry Brigades

2ND GUARDS BRIGADE

The 2nd Guards Brigade, on arrival in Malaya in October, 1947, adopted a new formation sign. This was an adaptation of the familiar badge of the war-time 33rd Guards Brigade, a vertical bayonet, point uppermost, set on a rectangle divided horizontally into three bands of the Household Brigade colours, dark blue and red.

On arrival in Malaya a Gurkha battalion came under the command of the Brigade, hence the addition to the Brigade sign of the kukri. This was made at the invitation of the Commander of the Gurkha Brigade, the sign of the Gurkha Brigade* being crossed kukris in white, set on a dark blue square.

---

* See page 62.

17TH INFANTRY BRIGADE

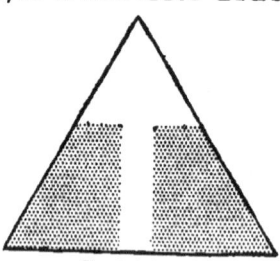

First Style Badge

The badge of this Brigade was a yellow arrow set on a red triangle, the arrow-head forming the apex of the triangle. It is felt that the symbolism was contained in the red representing the Infantry, the yellow the desert, and the triangle the Nile Delta, for this formation was located, at the time of the adoption of the badge, in the Canal Zone. In 1952 the Brigade adopted a new badge, similar in motif but of a different design, a yellow arrow pointing upwards, set on a scarlet rectangle.

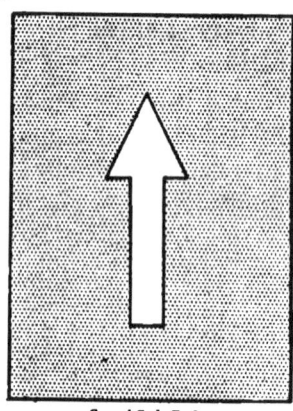

Second Style Badge

18TH INFANTRY BRIGADE

Similar in design to the badge adopted in Malaya by the 2nd Guards Brigade,* the badge of the 18th Infantry Brigade, also serving in Malaya, is composed of a crossed bayonet and kukri in white—the weapons outlined in brown—set on a red square background.

23RD BRITISH BRIGADE GROUP

One of the last British formations to serve in India, this Brigade Group, which was employed in 1946-47 on internal-security duties in the Punjab, adopted as its badge a dark blue shield divided by a yellow bar and surrounded with a yellow border, edged in black; in the top half of the shield were two and in the lower three yellow squares.

24TH INFANTRY BRIGADE

This Brigade wears the wartime badge of the 24th Independent Guards Brigade Group, a heraldic pinion in red picked out in dark blue, set on a dark blue rectangle.

---

* See page 63.

25TH INDEPENDENT INFANTRY BRIGADE

It was at the end of 1946 that the 2nd Division, then in the Far East, was ordered to re-form in North-West Europe, taking over the units of the 53rd (Welsh) Division. The 2nd Division Brigade Headquarters and the 4th, 5th and 6th Brigades also took part in this reorientation. The actual Brigades remained in the Far East and were redesignated the 24th, 25th and 26th Independent Infantry Brigades. At the time the 5th Brigade, composed of the 2nd Bn. The Royal Welch Fusiliers, the 2nd Bn. The Dorsetshire Regiment and the 1st Bn. The Cameron Highlanders, formed part of the British Commonwealth Occupation Force in Japan, but shortly afterwards was ordered to move to Malaya. The Brigade Commander, Brigadier R. S. McNaught, D.S.O. (who had commanded, in turn, each of the Brigades of the 2nd Division), decided to adopt a new badge for the 25th Independent Infantry Brigade, as the old 5th Brigade then became, for two reasons: firstly, to identify the formation with their old Division—hence the white crossed keys; and secondly, to commemorate the fact that they have been the only British Brigade to serve in Japan, the old 2nd Division badge was set between the arch of a Japanese "Torii," the sacred totem of the Japanese. The whole design was white on a black background.

27TH INFANTRY BRIGADE

This badge has a similarity to that of the (1939-45) wartime 3rd Division—a dark blue triangle having in the centre an inverted red triangle with the addition of three figures "9" (to add up to "27") in red on the three dark blue triangles formed by the design. The badge was worn by the 27th Brigade until it became part of the 40th Division in Hong Kong (when it adopted the Divisional badge*). It was this Brigade, with the designation "27th British Commonwealth Brigade," which was the first British formation to join the United Nations Forces in Korea, the Brigade being composed of the 1st Bn. The Middlesex Regiment, the 1st Bn. The Argyll and Sutherland Highlanders and the 32nd Australian Infantry Battalion.

---

* See page 58.

29TH INFANTRY BRIGADE

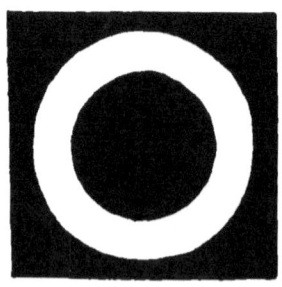

This Brigade's badge is a plain white ring set on a black square, the same as that worn by the 29th Independent Brigade Group during the 1939-45 War. The white ring was said to be the "O" of General Oliver Leese's name, for he was the first commander of the formation. The 29th Brigade* was mobilized in September, 1950, for service in Korea with the United Nations Force and consisted of the 1st Bn. The Royal Northumberland Fusiliers, the 1st Bn. The Gloucestershire Regiment, and the 1st Bn. The Royal Ulster Rifles, with supporting troops, including the 45th Field Regiment, R.A.

29TH BRITISH BRIGADE GROUP

In the 1939-45 War the 29th Brigade, originally an Independent Brigade Group, was subsequently incorporated into the 26th Indian Division, and became an Independent formation again in India after the disbandment of the Division. The Brigade was stationed at Deolali and was composed of 1st Bn. The Essex Regiment, the 1st Bn. The South Staffordshire Regiment and the 1st Bn. The Somerset Light Infantry. The Essex and South Staffordshire Battalions left India on 1st February, 1948, and the

---
* See First Commonwealth Division, page 59.

Somerset Light Infantry, the last British troops to leave India, embarked from Bombay on 28th February. The Brigade wore as its badge a four-leaved clover and stalk (taken from the badge of the 8th Indian Division) in yellow above the figures "29," also in yellow on a blue shield.

31ST INDEPENDENT INFANTRY BRIGADE

A jerboa (desert rat) in black on a scarlet oval is the badge of this Regular formation. The jerboa is of the same design as that which was the badge of the 4th Armoured Brigade which during the war served in the Middle East with the Eighth Army and in North-West Europe.

72ND BRITISH BRIGADE GROUP

This formation came into being in 1946 when the 36th Division was disbanded. The 72nd Brigade, which prior to its incorporation in the Division had as its sign a red circle on a square black background, did not, however, revert to this badge, but adopted the central part of the 36th Divisional sign—the interlocking portion of the two circles. This design, in yellow, was set on a blue shield with a narrow yellow border. The formation was stationed in Bangalore and was composed of the 1st Bn. The Essex Regiment, the 2nd Bn. The Royal Leicestershire Regiment, the 2nd Bn. The Manchester Regiment, and the 68th Field Regiment, R.A. Until it was disbanded, the Brigade Group was occupied on internal-security duties in Mysore. The 1st Essex had a detachment in the fort at Madras, and was the last British unit to be stationed in that ancient stronghold.

Airborne Forces

The well-known badge of the Airborne Forces, both Regular and T.A., is Bellerophon mounted on the winged horse, Pegasus, in pale blue set on a maroon square. The badge was adopted in 1941 with the formation of the Airborne Forces and was chosen because Bellerophon with his winged horse is the first recorded instance in Greek mythology of an airborne warrior, being famous for his slaying of the fire-breathing monster the Chimaera. Mounted on Pegasus with spear in hand, Bellerophon rode into the air, swooped down upon the monster and destroyed it.

Many stories have been written of the origin of Pegasus. The winged horse may symbolize the clouds, and the fight with the monster represents a thunderstorm, in which the heavenly rider destroyed the evil elements of the storm. The origin of the monster Chimaera is probably to be found in the eruptions of the volcano of this name in Greece. Though Bellerophon is sometimes represented as an armed warrior, he most commonly appears in art when mounted on Pegasus, as depicted in the Airborne Forces sign.

Training Brigade Groups

With the reorganization of the Infantry in 1947, regiments are now grouped. Training Brigade Groups were established, and men are liable for service in any unit within the Group. The Groups have been formed to group together the neighbouring County Regiments—*e.g.*, the East Anglian Group (composed of the Royal Norfolk, the Suffolk, the Essex and the Bedfordshire and Hertfordshire Regiments), the Wessex Group, the Highland Group, etc.— or groups of regiments having associated traditions— *e.g.*, the Light Infantry Brigade and the "Greenjackets" Group (60th Rifles (K.R.R.C.) and the Rifle Brigade).

These Training Brigade Groups have adopted distinctive signs which are worn below the shoulder title on the left sleeve.

YORKSHIRE AND NORTHUMBERLAND BRIGADE

The white rose of Yorkshire on a green stem with green leaves set on a scarlet square has been adopted as the badge of this Group, which is composed of all Yorkshire regiments (except K.O.Y.L.I., who form part of the Light Infantry Group) and the Royal Northumberland Fusiliers.

THE EAST ANGLIAN BRIGADE

This Brigade has adopted the same badge as that worn by East Anglia District, except that whereas the District badge depicts a Viking's head in white on a red shield, that of the Brigade is a yellow Viking on a blue shield.

THE MERCIAN BRIGADE

The Mercian Brigade is composed of the Cheshire and the Worcestershire Regiments and the South and North Staffordshire Regiments. The designation of this Brigade is historically suitable, for the Saxon Kingdom of Mercia* covered the English counties bordering the Welsh marches. The badge chosen for this Brigade is a shield of royal blue upon which is in gold a Saxon letter "M" for Mercia, below a Saxon crown within an outline of the shield in gold.

* The Kingdom of Mercia was founded by some Anglo-Saxon tribes about the year A.D. 585. Mercia lasted as a kingdom until A.D. 827, when it was captured by the Saxon Kingdom of Wessex and included in the territories of that kingdom. Mercia was the nearest Saxon kingdom to Wales, and its name was derived from the Saxon word for marshland or borderland, owing to its proximity to Wales.

The original Mercia consisted of the present county of Staffordshire, part and later all of Cheshire, Worcestershire and Shropshire, and small parts of West Derbyshire and Warwickshire.

THE WESSEX BRIGADE

The sign of the Wessex Group has been based on the arms of King Athelstan of Wessex,* who by combining the kingdoms of Wessex and Mercia became the first King of all England. Athelstan reigned from A.D. 925 to A.D. 937, and is buried at Malmesbury, Wilts. The sign is a cross in yellow set on four leaves, the upper and lower red, the side leaves in dark blue, set on a yellow diamond background. The Brigade is composed of the Devonshire, Gloucestershire, Dorset, Royal Hampshire and Wiltshire Regiments.†

---

* In the collection of Coats of Arms known as the "Domville Roll" (*circa* 1470) the arms of "Rex Athelstanus" include a "cross treflee or."

† The Somerset Light Infantry and Duke of Cornwall's Light Infantry are grouped in the Light Infantry Brigade.

THE LANCASTRIAN BRIGADE

The Lancastrian Training Brigade has taken as its badge the red rose of Lancaster set within a wreath of green laurel with red berries and tied at the base in a white knot. The design is set on a khaki background. This Group's badge may be identified with the cap-badge of the East Lancashire Regiment—which is the Lancastrian Group Training Battalion—the Group badge being composed of the laurel wreath and rose which are featured in the regimental cap-badge. The laurel wreath also features in the cap-badge of the South Lancashire Regiment whilst the rose of Lancaster appears also in the cap-badge of the Loyal Regiment (North Lancashire). The Group badge is therefore representative of the cap-badges of these three regiments of the Lancastrian Group.

HOME COUNTIES BRIGADE

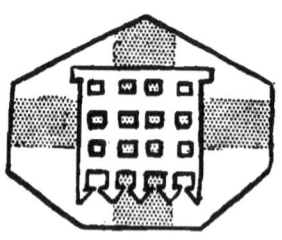

A yellow portcullis set on a red St. George's cross on a white heptagon. The symbolism of this badge is based on the seven regiments of this Group—the Queen's Royal Regiment, the Royal East Kent Regiment (The Buffs), the Royal Fusiliers, the East Surrey Regiment, the Royal Sussex Regiment, the Royal West Kent Regiment and the Middlesex Regiment—encircling the City of London, denoted by the red cross, and the City of Westminster, denoted by the portcullis. The St. George's cross and the portcullis are members of the arms of the two cities.

THE NORTH IRISH BRIGADE

A cut-out shamrock in dark green is worn by the members of the three Irish regiments of this training group—the Royal Inniskilling Fusiliers, the Royal Ulster Rifles, and the Royal Irish Fusiliers. The badge is similar to that worn by the 38th Infantry Brigade of the 78th Division (which was composed of battalions of the North Irish regiments) in North Africa and Italy during the late war.

THE MIDLAND BRIGADE

The badge of this Brigade is a red St. George's cross on a dark blue shield edged in dark green; in the royal blue sections of the shield are the Roman numerals in white of the four regiments of the Brigade: "VI" (The Royal Warwickshire Regiment), "X" (The Royal Lincolnshire Regiment), "XVII" (The Royal Leicestershire Regiment), and "XLV" (The Sherwood Foresters); the colours red and dark blue representing the three former regiments, whilst the dark green edge represents the Foresters.

THE "GREENJACKETS" GROUP

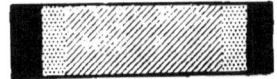

Composed of the King's Royal Rifle Corps and the Rifle Brigade, these regiments, which form the "Greenjackets" group, wear a distinctive flash, 2 in. by ¾ in., divided vertically with outer strips of black (the colour of the facings of the Rifle Brigade) and scarlet (the colour of the facings of the K.R.R.C.) and with a centre of rifle green.

Royal Artillery Formations (Regular Army)

2ND ARMY GROUP, R.A.

The symbol of Taurus (the Bull), the second sign of the zodiac, was adopted as the badge of this A.G.R.A. The sign is in white on a square black background.

3RD ARMY GROUP, R.A.

The barrel of an old-time cannon in yellow, picked out in black, set on a shield divided vertically into Gunner colours of red and dark blue, was the badge adopted in Palestine in 1947 by the 3rd Army Group Royal Artillery. The badge was later changed to a shield divided horizontally in two upper and lower blue bands with a central red band on which was the Roman numeral III in white.

5TH ARMY GROUP R.A. (A.A.)

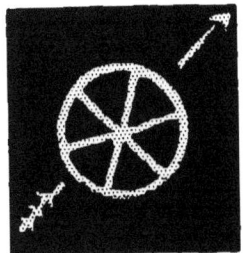

A red wheel, symbolizing mobility, and a red arrow pointing upwards, symbolic of the role of the formation, set on a blue square (thereby making use of the Gunner colours), is the badge adopted by this Regular A.G.R.A.

18TH TRAINING BRIGADE, R.A.

Symbolic of its role as a training formation, this Brigade wears a yellow torch of learning with seven flames with white high-lights and pale brown shading set on an evenly divided square background of Royal Artillery colours, top half red and lower half dark blue.

Royal Engineers (Regular Army)

FORTRESS ENGINEERS, GIBRALTAR

A representation of the Key of Gibraltar, in yellow, set on a dark blue diamond.

BOMB DISPOSAL UNITS, ROYAL ENGINEERS

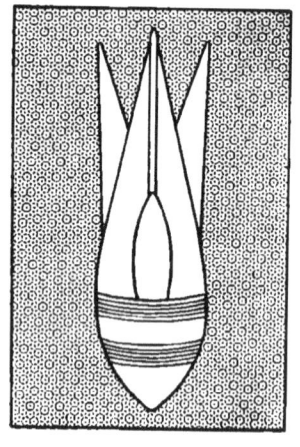

This badge, a yellow bomb, picked out in black and with two blue bands, set on a scarlet background 3 by 2 in., is worn on the left forearm, 6½ in. from the bottom of the sleeve, and was introduced in 1940* for wear by personnel of Bomb Disposal Units, R.E., to recognize the dangerous work on which they were employed. The badge is only worn by men on the strength of B.D. Units and it is withdrawn at the expiration of their term of duty.

* Army Council Instruction No. 1562 of 1940.

TRANSPORTATION UNITS R.E. (S.R.)

The half of a rolling stock wheel conjoined with the half of a capstan, the wheel so formed winged from the centre. This design in red set on a shield divided vertically, with the wheel portion set on a plain blue background and the section of the capstan set on a background divided by six wavy blue lines on a white ground. This appropriate badge is symbolic of the movement for which the Transportation Units of the Royal Engineers are responsible—railways and port operating, the red and blue colouring of the badge being the Corps Colours.

Royal Signals (Regular Army)
AIR FORMATION SIGNALS

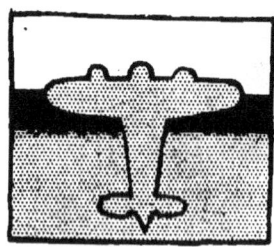

The silhouette of an aircraft in red—the Army colour—set on a background of dark green, symbolizing land light blue, the sky; and a dividing dark blue band, the sea

W.R.A.C. SIGNALS PERSONNEL

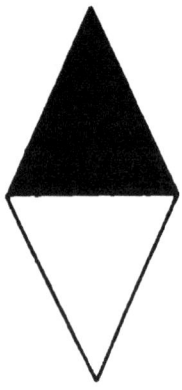

This diamond shaped badge divided horizontally, top half dark blue, and lower half white—the colours of the Royal Signals—is worn by all personnel of the Women' Royal Army Corps engaged on Signals duties.

R.A.S.C. Units (Regular Army)

ARMY FIRE SERVICE

The distinguishing badge of the Army Fire Service of the Royal Army Service Corps, which was introduced during the late war, comprises the words "Army Fire Service" in yellow set on a scarlet circle around a blue ring, in the centre of which is a yellow eight-pointed star on a scarlet background.

AIR DESPATCH GROUP, R.A.S.C.

A Dakota Aircraft in yellow on a royal blue square is the distinguishing badge of the Air Despatch Group Royal Army Service Corps, an organization first formed in April, 1944, with the task of maintenance by air and supply by air. For the former, personnel are trained as "Air Despatchers" flying in aircraft of Transport Command, R.A.F., for the dropping of supplies, petrol and ammunition by parachute. The second task involves the transport of supplies to airfields and the loading of Supply Aircraft.

WAR DEPARTMENT FLEET

The R.A.S.C. personnel of the War Department Fleet wear a miniature of the W.D. Fleet Ensign—a blue ensign, with a small union flag in the upper right-hand corner—and the crossed swords from the Army badge. The W.D. Fleet is composed of Water Transport Companies, Motor-Boat Companies and Boat Store Depots.

Territorial Army Formations

ARMY TROOPS (T.A.)

A shield evenly divided into Army colours—red, black, and red—with a yellow (gold) unsheathed Crusader's sword superimposed in the centre is the distinguishing badge, introduced in 1952, of all Army Troops Units of the Territorial Army.

21ST (NORTHERN) CORPS

The English lion in yellow and the Scottish lion rampant in yellow set on a shield evenly divided, horizontally, into three bars of Corps H.Q. colours —red, white and red.

23RD (SOUTHERN) CORPS

The twelfth sign of the zodiac, Capricornus, the sea goat, is the badge of this Corps. The goat is in brown with a yellow tail, set on a blue rectangle, the badge being adopted from the normal symbol for Capricorn as the nautical term "Twenty-three South" is the approximate latitude of the Tropic of Capricorn.

Territorial Army Divisions

The nine Divisions of the reconstituted Territorial Army which came into being on the 1st May, 1947, were : The 42nd (Lancashire); 43rd (Wessex); 44th (Home Counties); 50th (Northumbrian); 51st/52nd (Scottish)*; and 53rd (Welsh) Divisions; the 49th (West Riding and Midlands); and the 56th (London) Armoured Division and the 16th Airborne Division.

It will be seen that the T.A. did not break away from the now famous war-time badges—with the exception of the 56th (London) Armoured Division—and where the war-time badge was not retained in its original form the present badge resembles very closely that worn in the late war.

* Redesignated 51st (Highland) Division—see page 91—the 52nd (Lowland) Division was reconstituted in 1952.

42ND (LANCASHIRE) DIVISION (T.A.)

The 42nd (Lancashire) Division, which has taken the place of the 42nd (East Lancashire) and 55th (West Lancashire) Divisions, adopted as its new badge the red rose of Lancaster superimposed on the centre of a small white rectangle set on a larger red rectangle, thereby incorporating the former 42nd (East Lancs) Division badge with a portion of the old 55th (West Lancs) Division badge. The 42nd Division adopted during the 1939-45 War a badge of the same motif as was worn by the Division in the 1914-18 War—a diamond evenly divided, top half white, lower half red—the badge introduced in 1940 being a small white rectangle set on a larger red rectangle. The badge, one of the smallest formation badges, was only nine-tenths of an inch in diameter. This badge continued to be worn by the 42nd Armoured Division, which was formed in 1941 by conversion of the 42nd (East Lancs) Infantry Division. When this Armoured Division was disbanded in 1943 the Divisional Engineers remained as a complete unit and became the 42nd Assault Regiment, R.E. (later redesignated 42nd Armoured Engineer Regiment), and throughout their service continued to wear the old 42nd (East Lancs) Divisional badge. This badge, now enlarged to one and nine-tenths of an inch in diameter, has been retained by the new 42nd (Lancashire) Division. In the centre of the badge is the conventional flower of the red rose of Lancaster. This is a portion of the badge of the 55th (West Lancs) Division as worn in both the 1914-18 and the 1939-45 Wars. The rose as depicted in that badge has five petals inside and five outside.

43RD (WESSEX) DIVISION (T.A.)

The 43rd (Wessex) Division has retained the pre-war and war-time badge of the formation, the ancient emblem of the kings of Wessex, an heraldic wyvern* in yellow on a dark blue square.†

---

* The wyvern was featured in the badge of The West Somerset Yeomanry.
† In the late war the 43rd (Wessex) Division saw active service in North-West Europe with 21st Army Group (1944-45).

44TH (HOME COUNTIES) DIVISION (T.A.)

The 44th (Home Counties) Division has adopted a new badge which incorporates the war-time badge of the formation, a scarlet oval with a white border worn horizontally and also the badge originally adopted by East Kent District, which later became Kent District, and is now worn by Home Counties District. This badge took the form of a shield with a narrow white border within which was depicted Dover Castle in black silhouette, set on a green foreground above the white cliffs of Dover and a blue sea. This badge is now superimposed on the centre of the scarlet oval of the war-time 44th Division to form the badge of the 44th (Home Counties) Division (T.A.).*

---

* The 44th (Home Counties) Division saw service with the B.E.F. in 1940. It went to the Middle East in 1942 and formed part of the Eighth Army at El Alamein, but was later disbanded on the reorganization of the Middle East Force

49TH (WEST RIDING AND MIDLAND) ARMOURED DIVISION (T.A.)

The 49th (West Riding and Midland) Armoured Division (T.A.), which is the lineal descendant of the pre-war 49th (West Riding) Division, has now included the word "Midlands" in its sub-title, for it partly covers the pre-war recruiting areas of the former 46th (North Midland) and 48th (South Midland) T.A. Divisional Areas. The Division has retained the second design of the famous war-time Polar bear badge of the 49th. This badge was adopted whilst the Division was in Iceland (1940-43).*

50TH (NORTHUMBRIAN) DIVISION (T.A.)

The 50th (Northumbrian) Division has retained its 1939-45 War badge, the well-known red capital "Ts" (for the Rivers Tyne and Tees) set on a black square.†

---

* The Division, which had served in Norway in 1940, later served in N.W. Europe (1944-45).

† In the late war the 50th (Northumbrian) Division served with the B.E.F. in 1940; in the Western Desert, 1941-43; in the invasion of Sicily in 1943; and in France and Belgium in 1944.

51ST (HIGHLAND) DIVISION (T.A.)

The 51st/52nd (Scottish) Division, which amalgamated the former 51st (Highland) and 52nd (Lowland) T.A. Divisions, was subsequently redesignated 51st (Highland) Division, thereby reverting to the pre-1939 title of one of Scotland's T.A. Divisions, and keeping alive a divisional designation both numerical and geographical which had won fame in the two great wars of 1914-18 and 1939-45.

The Division has retained the badge it bore in both the 1914-18 and 1939-45 Wars,* namely, the red letters "HD" conjoined within a red circle set on a square blue background.

---

* The 51st Division served with the B.E.F. in 1940. It was re-formed (after the loss of two Brigades at St. Valery-en-Caux in May, 1940), and later served with the Eighth Army in the Western Desert, in the invasion of Sicily, and in North-West Europe from Normandy to the Elbe.

52ND (LOWLAND) DIVISION (T.A.)

The white cross of St. Andrew of Scotland on a blue shield within a narrow black border, is the badge of the 52nd (Lowland) Division (T.A.), which prior to its re-formation in 1952 was worn by the 155th (Lowland) Independent Brigade Group (T.A.), which had continued to wear the Divisional badge* on the reconstitution of the Territorial Army in 1947. This badge is now also worn by the 30th (Lowland) Armoured Brigade which had since 1947 worn their own distinguishing badge.†

---

* In the 1914-18 War the Divisional sign of the 52nd (Lowland) Division, designed by Major-General John Hill, C.B., D.S.O., was a small white cross of St. Andrew set on a blue shield. On the centre of the cross was a thistle. The shield was set in the angle of a letter "L" for Lowland. This Divisional badge continued to be worn by the 52nd (Lowland) Division (T.A.) between the wars. In 1940, however, it was changed to that depicted above, and to this was added a scroll below with the word "Mountain" in white on a blue ground when the Division adopted that operational role.

† See page 97.

53RD (WELSH) DIVISION (T.A.)

The 53rd (Welsh) Division has also kept its war-time badge,* a red "W", the base of the letter resting on a red horizontal bar, the design set on a khaki background. There are several explanations of this badge, and I have yet to discover the real symbolism. It has been said that the "W" stood for Wales and for Wilson—Major-General B. T. Wilson was the Divisional Commander at the time of its adoption—also that the design was symbolic of a Bardic crown; or again that it represented the traditional tall hat of the Woman of Wales, and also that it was symbolic of the firm base of the attack (the horizontal), the spearhead of the attack (the centre inverted "V" of the "W"), and the outflanking movements (the side portions of the "W").

---

* The 53rd (Welsh) Division formed part of 21st Army Group in the operations in North-West Europe, 1944-45.

56TH (LONDON) ARMOURED DIVISION (T.A.)

Badge worn 1947-1950

The original 1st London Division (T.F.), which during the 1914-18 War was redesignated 56th (1st London) Division (T.A.), remained so known until 1936, when it became the London Division. It reverted to its numerical title of "56" in 1939. With the reconstitution of the T.A. in 1947, the formation, which had been an Infantry Division during the 1939-45 War, was re-formed as an Armoured Division, and adopted a new badge which incorporated a portion (the sword) which was reminiscent of the Divisional sign of the 1914-18 War. During the 1939-45 War the formation bore as its badge a black cat—Dick Whittington's cat—set on a scarlet rectangle. The new badge is symbolic of its new role—a knight's helmet, in blue, superimposed on a sword in red, the design set on a white rectangle; the sword being taken from that which appears in the dexter quarter of the arms of the City of London; and the knight's helmet associating the formation with its armoured role following the fashion set during the 1939-45 War by Armoured Divisions—for example, the knight's helmet of the 2nd Armoured Division, the mailed fist of the 6th Armoured Division, and the charging knight of VIII Corps. The red sword which is incorporated in the badge has made its appearance in other badges of formations associated with London—for example, the original 1st Anti-Aircraft Division and London District—whilst the badge of the Division in the 1914-18 War was a plain vertical red sword, point uppermost.

In 1950 the Divisional badge was changed. The Black Cat badge which was worn in the 1939-45 War* was reintroduced with the addition of a red sword—taken from

Present Badge of the Division

---

* The 56th Division served in Persia and Iraq force, and in Palestine between 1942-43. It took part in the landings at Anzio and Salerno and served throughout the campaign in Italy, 1943-45.

the Divisional sign of World War I and from the badge adopted in 1947 (illustrated on page 94)—set, point uppermost, on the back of the cat.

Armoured Brigades (T.A.)

9TH INDEPENDENT ARMOURED BRIGADE (T.A.)

This Brigade has retained the war-time badge of the 9th Armoured Brigade—a white horse set on a green semicircle.

23RD INDEPENDENT ARMOURED BRIGADE (T.A.)

This formation wears the war-time badge of the 23rd Armoured Brigade—a black liver bird, in its beak an olive branch, set on a white circle.

30TH (LOWLANDS) INDEPENDENT ARMOURED BRIGADE (T.A.)

This Scottish T.A. Armoured formation adopted a symbolic badge.* The head of a white Clydesdale horse, representative of the Lowlands—armoured, to link with the Brigade's role—set upon the white St. Andrew's cross of Scotland on a blue background, the reins embroidered with three X's making the Roman figure for the Brigade number—thirty.

---

* This Brigade now (1952) wears the badge of the 52nd (Lowland) Division (see page 92).

Infantry Brigades (T.A.)

107TH (ULSTER) INDEPENDENT BRIGADE GROUP (T.A.)

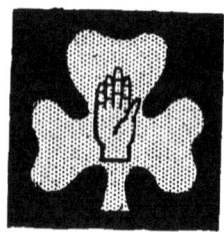

This Northern Ireland Independent Brigade Group has adopted as its badge the red hand of Ulster superimposed on a green shamrock set on a khaki square, the badge thereby incorporating the national emblems of Ireland—the shamrock, which was worn during the war by the 38th Infantry Brigade, made up of Irish units in the 78th Division, and the badge of Ulster, which was the Divisional sign of the 36th (Ulster) Division in the 1914-18 War and was also worn as a regimental sign by several Ulster units during the late war. This T.A. Brigade has its Headquarters in Belfast.

161st INDEPENDENT INFANTRY BRIGADE GROUP (T.A.)

A representation of Boadicea in her war chariot drawn by two prancing horses in black set on a red rectangle has been adopted by this T.A. Infantry Brigade, which is recruited in Norfolk, Suffolk and Essex. The badge has been chosen because Boadicea was the wife of Prasutagus, King of the Iceni, who populated East Anglia—the present recruiting area of the Brigade—and it was at Camalodunum (Colchester) that, following the death of the King, Boadicea, leading the Iceni, defeated the Romans in A.D. 62.

162ND INDEPENDENT INFANTRY BRIGADE GROUP (T.A.)

The sign adopted by this Brigade is representative of the three major units of the Brigade, the 1st Bn. The Hertfordshire Regiment (T.A.), the 5th Bn. The Bedfordshire and Hertfordshire Regiment (T.A.), and the 5th Bn. The Northamptonshire Regiment (T.A.). The centre-piece of the sign in black is the castle and key, taken from the cap-badge of the Northamptonshire Regiment. The amber pack-of-cards type of heart is representative of the Hertfordshire Regiment, whilst the colours, black and amber, are those of the Bedfordshire and Hertfordshire Regiment.*

---

* See page 149.

264TH (SCOTTISH) BEACH BRIGADE (T.A.)

This Territorial Army Brigade adopted a small replica of the war-time badge of the Beach Groups, a fouled anchor in red on a pale blue background within a red circle, set in the centre of a white cross of St. Andrew on a dark blue shield—the former badge of the 52nd (Lowland) Division.*

---

* This Brigade now (1952) wears the badge of the 52nd (Lowland) Division (see page 92).

Royal Artillery Formations (T.A.)

84TH ARMY GROUP, R.A. (T.A.)

The design of the badge adopted by this A.G.R.A. was drawn up by Sir Thomas Innes, Lord Lyon King of Arms, in February, 1947, a month after the raising of the formation. The Headquarters of the A.G.R.A. is in Aberdeen, and its units are spread out from Banff and Fraserburgh in the north to Edinburgh and Glasgow in the south. The badge depicts a white triple tower, suggesting Aberdeen, for a similar tower forms part of the crest of the city. The galley represents Clan Chattan, which covers a great part of the Highlands where galleys of many types and colours are featured in the armorial bearings. The two St. Andrew's flags denote the over-all connection with Scotland. The flags fly so that they always face the rear when worn on the sleeve on the principle that the A.G.R.A. is invariably moving forward. The design is set on a square background evenly divided into Gunner colours—top half red and the lower half dark blue.

85TH ARMY GROUP, R.A. (T.A.)

This Scottish A.G.R.A. wears as its badge a yellow gun of traditional model set on a blue-and-white diced diagonal band across a square, the top left-hand position being red and the lower right portion dark blue, the Royal Artillery colours.

86TH ARMY GROUP, R.A. (T.A.)

This Territorial A.G.R.A. wears the war-time badge of 6th A.G.R.A.—the sixth sign of the zodiac in white set in a black square. The badge was introduced to 86th A.G.R.A. by the Commander, Brigadier J. St. C. Holbrook, C.B.E., M.C., who commanded the 6th A.G.R.A. in Italy.

87TH ARMY GROUP, R.A. (FIELD) (T.A.)

This Lancashire T.A. Gunner formation has adopted as its sign the war-time badge of the 55th (West Lancashire) Division (T.A.)—the red rose of Lancaster, with green stem and leaves, set on a khaki circle.

88TH ARMY GROUP, R.A. (FIELD) (T.A.)

A field gun in gold, of the same pattern as in the Royal Artillery cap-badge, below the figures "88," also in gold, set on a diamond background evenly divided vertically into Gunner colours—dark blue and red.

89TH ARMY GROUP, R.A. (FIELD) (T.A.)

A silver horseshoe and the Royal Artillery grenade in gold set on a square green background.

90TH ARMY GROUP, R.A. (FIELD) (T.A.)

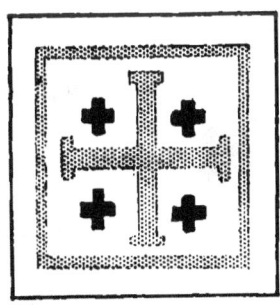

A cross crosslet in dull red, with four small dark blue crosses set within the arms of the main cross, within a dull red square on a square white background.

91ST ARMY GROUP, R.A. (FIELD) (T.A.)

The badge of this A.G.R.A. is the head of a deer in gold set on a Light Infantry green square—the Territorial Army colours, yellow and green—the deer being chosen as representative of the red deer of Devon and Somerset, the counties in which the A.G.R.A. is recruited.

92ND ARMY GROUP, R.A. (A.A.) (T.A.)

A Falcon poised on the gloved hand of a falconer in white, set on a square background evenly divided top half red, lower half dark blue, the Royal Artillery colours, was the badge of the 92nd A.G.R.A. (A.A.) (T.A.)—a formation now in "suspended animation." The badge is, however, still worn by the 321st H.A.A. Regiment, R.A. (T.A.), one of the units which formed the A.G.R.A.

93RD ARMY GROUP, R.A. (T.A.)

The badge adopted by this formation is the R.A. grenade collar-badge in yellow above a scroll bearing the figures "93"—the A.G.R.A.'s number—set on a rectangular background evenly divided into R.A. colours of red and dark blue. Below the badge are the yellow letters "AA"—one letter set on the red portion of the background, one letter set on the blue. This A.G.R.A. has now been redesignated 93rd A.A. Brigade, R.A.

94TH ARMY GROUP, R.A. (A.A.) (T.A.)

This formation was made up of R.A. (T.A.) units in Lancashire and Cheshire, hence the adoption of the badge—a shield divided horizontally into red and dark blue, Gunner colours. On the upper red portion the Cheshire garb (a wheatsheaf) in yellow picked out in black. On the lower blue portion the red rose of Lancaster.

95TH ARMY GROUP, R.A. (A.A.) (T.A.)

This Anti-Aircraft A.G.R.A. adopted an appropriate design of a red shell with blue fuse and driving bands, pointing upwards, set on a blue shield, with a semicircle of white at the top, in which is placed an aircraft silhouette in blue, indicative of the A.A. shell in flight through the sky to its target, the aircraft in the cloud.

This A.G.R.A. has now become the 95th Anti-Aircraft Brigade, R.A.

96TH ARMY GROUP, R.A. (A.A.) (T.A.)

The badge of this Liverpool T.A. Gunner formation appropriately depicts the famous Liver Buildings (in yellow), as representative of the city, set on a red and blue background—Gunner colours—with yellow wavy lines on the lower dark blue portion representative of the River Mersey.

97TH ARMY GROUP, R.A. (A.A.) (T.A.)

This London Territorial R.A. formation has adopted a silhouette of the statue of Eros in red set on a dark blue background, thereby linking its association with London with the Royal Artillery colours.

100TH ARMY GROUP, R.A. (A.A.) (T.A.)

This A.G.R.A. was made up of three Hampshire T.A. units and one from Wiltshire. Hence the choice of the badge. In the upper portion of the shield the Hampshire rose, as used in the badge of the Royal Hampshire Regiment and in the arms of the county, and four pale green and four white bars taken from the shield of the arms of the county of Wiltshire. The lower portion of the shield is divided into the red and dark blue Gunner colours.

101ST COAST BRIGADE, R.A. (T.A.)

A white castle gateway, picked out in dark blue and with portcullis lowered, set in a circle against a green background in the upper half of the circle, the lower half being dark blue with two wavy white bars. The badge is described heraldically as "Standing between land and sea, a gateway with portcullis lowered"—symbolic of the role of coast defence units, barring the way of seaborne invaders.

102ND COAST BRIGADE, R.A. (T.A.)
104TH COAST BRIGADE, R.A. (T.A.)

A yellow setting sun on a red sky sinking into a blue sea—the Gunner colours—framed in a white letter "W" set on a khaki background. The sign links the formation with Wallasey, its Headquarters, and with Western Command.

On the reorganization of the Coast Brigades of the T.A., when 104th Coast Brigade was disbanded, this badge was adopted by 102nd Coast Brigade, R.A. (T.A.).

105TH COAST BRIGADE, R.A. (T.A.)

This Scottish T.A. Coast Artillery formation has adopted as its badge the heraldic lion rampant of Scotland in yellow, as on the Scottish Command badge, set on a square background divided diagonally into the Gunner colours of red and blue.

Royal Engineer Formations (T.A.)

21ST ENGINEER GROUP (T.A.)

A shield bearing the colours of the Royal Engineer flash with the figures "21" in royal blue on the central scarlet bar.

22ND ENGINEER GROUP (T.A.)

The badge of Northumbrian District*—St. Oswald's shield of Northumbria of eight yellow and red vertical bars set on a royal blue background on a blue square—has been adopted by this T.A. formation, with the addition of the Royal Engineers' collar-badge—a seven-flamed grenade above the scroll bearing the motto "Ubique" in yellow set in the centre of the shield.

* See page 38.

23RD ENGINEER GROUP (T.A.)

The Royal Engineer colours set in the same manner as the Corps flag, flash and tie, royal blue and red diagonals on a shield with a royal blue border.

24TH ENGINEER GROUP (T.A.)

First Style Badge

This Territorial Army Engineer Group, which has its H.Q. in Liverpool, first adopted as its sign a patch of Royal Engineer colours—red with two vertical royal blue stripes. In the centre was a small reproduction of the former badge of the 55th (West Lancashire) Division (T.A.)—the red rose of Lancaster with green stem and leaves set on a khaki circular background; the rose having five petals inside and five outside with five leaves on either side of the stem, thereby repeating the divisional number "55."

Second Style Badge

In 1952 the Group adopted a new badge which is more appropriate, as the formation comprises Sapper Territorial units from both Lancashire and Staffordshire. The new badge depicts the red rose of Lancashire with green stem and leaves, above a white Staffordshire knot, set on a Sapper blue square.

25TH ENGINEER GROUP (T.A.)

The three seaxes of Essex in white (denoting the county where the territorial units composing the Group are located) set on a rectangle of R.E. colours.

26TH ENGINEER GROUP (T.A.)

A Wiltshire white horse* set on a cobalt blue background —the same colour blue as used for R.E. vehicle marking— is the badge of this T.A. Engineer formation which has its Headquarters near Salisbury.

27TH ENGINEER GROUP (T.A.)

A representation in yellow of the seven-flamed grenade of the Royal Engineers above a scroll bearing the Sappers' motto "Ubique," set on a royal blue shield.

---

* There are six white horses cut in the Wiltshire Downs. The design of this badge, however, bears a close resemblance to the Westbury white horse at Bratton, near Westbury.

Canadian Army Formation Signs

25TH CANADIAN INFANTRY BRIGADE

Originally designated "Canadian Army Special Force," made up of a Brigade Group, this force—now designated the 25th Canadian Infantry Brigade—was the Dominion contribution to the United Nations Forces in Korea. The Brigade, which is composed of The Royal Canadian Regiment, Princess Patricia's Canadian Light Infantry and the Royal 22ᵉ Regiment, forms part of the First Commonwealth Division.* The formation badge, or "patch" as it is called in the Canadian Army, is a red shield, on it the word "Canada," and a maple leaf in gold, the national emblem being encircled with a white laurel wreath, symbolic of the United Nations.

---

* See page 59.

27TH CANADIAN INFANTRY BRIGADE

The Canadian Brigade Group now forming part of the British Army of the Rhine, and composed of the 1st Canadian Infantry Battalion, 1st Canadian Rifle Battalion, 1st Canadian Highland Battalion, with attached troops, wears as its badge a French grey shield with the word "Canada" in gold set in the upper portion. The three infantry battalions have their own distinctive badges,* and the Brigade "flash" is worn by the Headquarters Staff and all other troops under command.

---

* See pages 118–120.

1st CANADIAN INFANTRY BATTALION

A French grey shield with the word "Canada" in gold set above a scarlet unsheathed bayonet, point uppermost, in the centre of the shield is worn by the 1st Canadian Infantry Battalion, which has drawn its personnel from the Loyal Edmonton Regiment, the Hastings and Prince Edward Regiment, the Carleton and York Regiment from New Brunswick, the Algonquin Regiment from North Bay, Ontario, and Les Fusiliers Mont-Royal.

1st CANADIAN HIGHLAND BATTALION

A bright green and red thistle set below the word "Canada" in gold on a French grey shield distinguishes the 1st Canadian Highland Battalion, which is composed of men from the Seaforth Highlanders of Canada from Vancouver, the 48th Highlanders of Canada from Toronto, the Black Watch (Royal Highland Regiment) of Canada from Montreal, the North Nova Scotia Regiment, and the Canadian Scottish Regiment from British Columbia.

1st CANADIAN RIFLE BATTALION

A black rifle bugle with white strings, set in the centre of a French grey shield below the word "Canada" in gold, is the badge of the 1st Canadian Rifle Battalion, which is composed of Officers, N.C.Os. and men drawn from the Queen's Own Rifles of Canada from Toronto, the Victoria Rifles of Canada from Montreal, the Regina Rifle Regiment, the Royal Winnipeg Rifles, and the Royal Hamilton Light Infantry.

Australian Army Formation Signs

The colour patches introduced during the 1914-18 War to distinguish the Australian formations were abolished in 1950 and have now been replaced by formation signs. Fifteen formation signs have been approved, all of different designs, woven on washable material, each badge being 2½ in. square. Australian troops wear the formation sign of their particular formation irrespective of where they may be serving at the time.

The introduction of these new formation signs was found necessary because of the confusion, during the late war, due to factors which had not been envisaged when the colour-patch system of identification was originally adopted. The original colour patches identified units by the variation of shape and colours of the patches and this method was satisfactory whilst the continuity of numbering of units was maintained.

The new badges now adopted are more in keeping with the general style of formation badge adopted by the British Army. With the exception of Eastern and Northern Territory Commands, those adopted by Commands are based on the badges of the States forming the Commonwealth, which are incorporated in the shield of the arms of Australia which were adopted in 1912. Two war-time badges (those of the 1st Australian Armoured Division and the 4th Armoured Brigade) have been reintroduced for the present 1st and 2nd Armoured Brigades.

ARMY HEADQUARTERS

The Imperial Crown, in red and yellow, surmounted by a lion, superimposed on a shield evenly divided horizontally. The top half red, the lower half blue. The whole set on a yellow square background.

NORTHERN COMMAND
(Queensland)

The Imperial Crown superimposed on a royal blue Maltese cross, based on the badge of Queensland (taken from the third quarter of the arms of Australia) set on a white square background.

NORTHERN TERRITORY COMMAND

A black buffalo's head picked out in white and yellow, and with white horns, in the centre of a yellow circle on a green square with yellow edges, has been adopted by the Northern Territory Command.

CENTRAL COMMAND
(SOUTH AUSTRALIA)

Formerly the 4th Military District, this Command has adopted as its badge a piping shrike (magpie) in black and white, with wings outstretched, set on a yellow circle with a narrow black border on a light brown square, being an adaptation of the badge of South Australia in the fourth quarter of the Commonwealth's arms.

EASTERN COMMAND
(NEW SOUTH WALES)

A scarlet waratah on a white square. (The waratah is an Australian genus of trees and shrubs, the latter bearing large heads of crimson flowers.)

WESTERN COMMAND

The black swan of Western Australia set on a yellow ground, taken from the fifth quartering of the arms of the Commonwealth.

3RD MILITARY DISTRICT (VICTORIA)

The constellation of the Southern Cross, white stars set on a blue shield surmounted by a crown, in white picked out in blue on a light blue square, the badge being adopted from that of Victoria which appears in the second quarter of the arms of Australia.

TASMANIA COMMAND

Originally designated the 6th Military District, Tasmania Command wears Tasmania's badge, a lion rampant in red picked out in brown on a gold shield set on a light brown square, the badge being based on that in the sixth quarter of Australia's arms.

2ND INFANTRY DIVISION

Crossed bayonets in white below the figure "2" in white, set on a scarlet square.

3RD INFANTRY DIVISION

Crossed bayonets in yellow below the badge of the Australian military forces,* in yellow, and above the Roman numeral III, also in yellow, set on a red square.

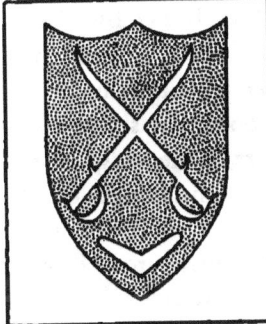

1ST INFANTRY BRIGADE GROUP

Crossed swords, in gold, set above a boomerang in gold, on a red shield set on a light khaki square.

11TH INFANTRY BRIGADE

Two vertical red arrows within an eleven-pointed star, in white, set on a red square.

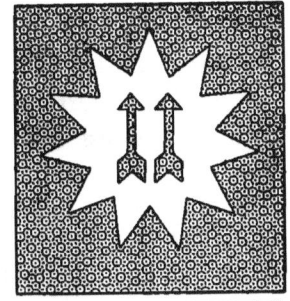

---

* The badge of the Australian military forces is based on the badge of the First Regiment of Australian Light Horse which served with the Imperial Forces in South Africa (1899-1902) and which had been designed to represent a Trophy of Army swords and bayonets surrounding the Imperial Crown.

13TH INFANTRY BRIGADE

A green shield set on a blue square, with a mailed arm and hand grasping a dagger, in white, picked out in green, set on a base divided diagonally into three red and three blue bars.

1ST ARMOURED BRIGADE

A red alligator, superimposed on a green palm tree, and above a black boomerang set on a yellow square, is the badge of this Brigade which is based on the vehicle-marking badge of the 4th Australian Armoured Brigade raised in 1943, and which subsequently served in New Guinea, New Britain and Borneo.

2ND ARMOURED BRIGADE

A mailed forearm and hand grasping a raised battleaxe, in black, set on a yellow square. This Brigade has adopted the badge of the 1st Australian Armoured Division, which was raised in 1941 and later redesignated (in 1943) the 1st Armoured Brigade Group, which fought in New Guinea.

G.H.Q. PAKISTAN

Crossed swords, with curved blades in silver, with golden hilts, below a silver crescent moon and five-pointed star set on a dark green shield is the badge adopted by G.H.Q. Pakistan.

HONG KONG DEFENCE FORCE

An equilateral triangle, divided vertically into three even (at the base) portions—blue, yellow and red—is the distinctive flash of the Hong Kong Defence Force.

THE KING'S OWN MALTA REGIMENT

The four battalions of the King's Own Malta Regiment wear distinctive cloth patches on the sleeve; each patch is of a different geometrical shape, but all are evenly divided into red and white portions.

Regimental Badges and Shoulder Flashes

The practice of wearing regimental badges and flashes dates back many years before the introduction of the formation badges which were first adopted in the form of Army, Corps and Divisional signs in the 1914-18 War.

Patches, flashes and strips of ribbon or cloth (mainly in regimental colours) as a means of identification have been introduced and adopted gradually, and, in some instances, date from a specific campaign or operation following the introduction of khaki drill and later service dress. Coloured regimental distinguishing patches were worn during the South African War, and again in the 1914-18 War, especially when three or four battalions of the same regiment were brigaded together.

The wearing of such patches, etc., has been continued throughout the years, and, although originally most of these distinguishing signs were unofficial, the position has, in many cases, been regularized and a number of regiments are now authorized to wear such distinguishing marks on battledress. This practice is particularly prevalent in the case of converted units, mainly Territorial Army—R.A.C. and Heavy and Light A.A. Regiments which were formed from Yeomanry Cavalry, and Infantry Battalions. In a number of cases a definite badge has been adopted, but the majority of these regimental signs are strips and patches of regimental colours, or geometrical designs incorporating such.

ROYAL ARMOURED CORPS

The Royal Armoured Corps badge,* woven in yellow on a khaki background, is worn by all other ranks of the R.A.C. (including the Royal Tank Regiment) on the left arm of the battledress blouse or service dress jacket (and will be worn on No. 1 Dress when issued), immediately below the formation badge or, when worn by N.C.Os., immediately above the rank chevrons.

---

* The Royal Armoured Corps was formed in 1939 by the grouping of the mechanized regiments of Cavalry of the Line and the Royal Tank Regiment. Later the remaining horsed Cavalry regiments and certain Yeomanry and other T.A. units were included in the Corps, and, in December, 1940, and January, 1941, the war-time raised regiments of Hussars, Dragoons and Lancers (22nd and 25th Dragoons, 23rd and 26th Hussars and 24th and 27th Lancers). The badge adopted for the R.A.C. was the mailed gauntlet, with a billet on the wrist bearing the inscription "R.A.C." (representing the hard punch of the Armour) and two concentric circles with arrow-heads (representing pincer movements), the design being surmounted by the Imperial Crown.

65th Training Regiment

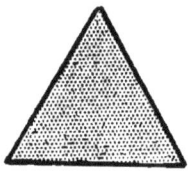
66th Training Regiment

ROYAL ARMOURED CORPS— TRAINING REGIMENTS

The four Training Regiments of the Royal Armoured Corps in the United Kingdom wear, as distinguishing badges on the battledress sleeve, a small felt inverted triangle, each Regiment having a different colour:

    65th Training Regiment, R.A.C. ... ... Red
    66th Training Regiment, R.A.C. ...   Yellow
    67th Training Regiment, R.A.C. ... ... Blue
    68th Training Regiment, R.A.C.   White

67th Training Regiment

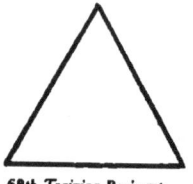
68th Training Regiment

4TH/7TH ROYAL DRAGOON GUARDS

This Regular regiment wears on the left arm, below the formation badge,* a diamond-shaped flash in regimental colours—black, gold and dull red.

This regimental flash was adopted in 1939. At the outbreak of war the 4th/7th Royal Dragoon Guards were the Divisional Cavalry Regiment of the 2nd Division and on mobilization proceeded to France with the B.E.F. It was expected that when actual fighting commenced the regiment would not, for security reasons, be permitted to wear badges or numerals, and therefore, in order to have some form of regimental distinguishing sign—considered essential for recognition purposes—it was decided to adopt a regimental flash of design and colouring similar to that which was painted on the regiment's steel helmets. This was done and the regiment continues to wear this distinctive flash.

---

* See page 162.

9TH QUEEN'S ROYAL LANCERS

The regimental flash of the 9th Lancers worn on the battledress was first adopted in 1940 when the Royal Armoured Corps distinguishing arm-of-service strip was introduced (a strip 2 in. long by ¼ in. deep evenly divided into two portions, yellow and red). As these R.A.C. colours were similar to the regimental colours of the 9th Lancers—scarlet and gold—it was decided to wear one above the other, with the R.A.C. flash on top. When the R.A.C. flash was abolished in 1947 it was decided to continue to wear both flashes. This course was adopted because to have removed one flash only would have made it appear that the regiment had failed to remove the R.A.C. flash and were wearing it the wrong way round.

THE 13TH/18TH ROYAL HUSSARS (QUEEN MARY'S OWN)

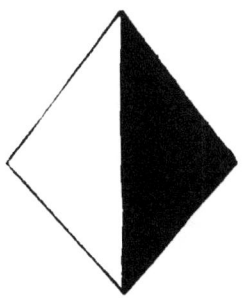

A regimental flash in the shape of a diamond divided vertically, one half dark blue, the other half white—the regimental colours—is worn by all ranks of the 13th/18th Royal Hussars on the left sleeve of battledress with the white portion to the front.

14TH/20TH KING'S HUSSARS

This regiment wears a small metal arm badge*—a miniature of the renowned badge of the Gurkha regiments —two crossed kukris in white metal. The badge was adopted in January, 1947, as a recognition of the close association and comradeship of the regiment with the Gurkha battalions of the 43rd Lorried Infantry Brigade with which they served from 1941 to 1945.

* See page 163.

ROYAL TANK REGIMENT

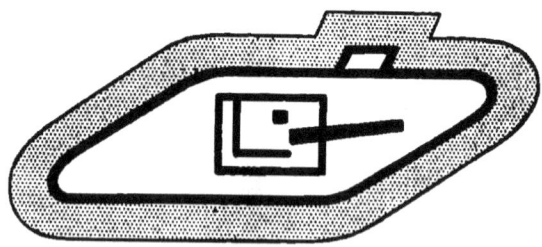

All ranks of the Royal Tank Regiment wear the Tank arm badge in addition to the Royal Armoured Corps* arm badge, which is worn on the left arm. The Tank badge is worn on the right upper arm below the formation badge and above the rank chevrons.

This Tank arm badge was authorized in March, 1917, for wear on the upper sleeve by all ranks of the Heavy Branch of the Machine Gun Corps, which in July, 1917, became the Tank Corps, later becoming The Royal Tank Corps in recognition of its service in the 1914-18 War. This arm badge became the basis for the regimental badge worn today by the Royal Tank Regiment.†

---

* When the Royal Tank Corps became part of the then newly formed Royal Armoured Corps in April, 1939, its title was changed to Royal Tank Regiment.
† The badge of the Royal Tank Regiment is: "Within a laurel wreath, surmounted by a crown, an early model tank; on the bottom of the wreath a scroll inscribed 'Fear Naught' " (*vide* "Regimental Badges" by Major T. J. Edwards, M.B.E., F.R.Hist.S. (Gale & Polden Ltd., 1951).

THE ROYAL GLOUCESTERSHIRE HUSSARS

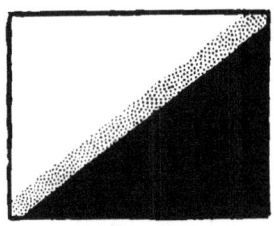

This regiment of yeomanry, which was raised in 1830 and is now a unit of the Royal Armoured Corps, wears a regimental flash 2½ in. by 1¾ in. The flash is divided diagonally by a ¼-in. maroon strip. The left-hand portion of the flash is yellow and the right-hand royal blue.

THE FIFE AND FORFAR YEOMANRY

A rectangular arm flash composed of a St. Andrew cross incorporating the regimental colours—yellow diagonal set across a red diagonal—on a dark blue background, has been adopted by this Royal Armoured Corps Regiment of the T.A.

79TH HEAVY ANTI-AIRCRAFT REGIMENT, ROYAL ARTILLERY

This Regular Heavy Anti-Aircraft Regiment was formed in Malta in 1936 as the 7th A.A. Brigade, later redesignated Regiment, then Heavy A.A. Regiment, and finally numbered 79th. From 1936 until the outbreak of war in 1939, the Regiment was entirely responsible for the preparations for the island's Anti-Aircraft Defence, both the manning of war stations and the training of personnel of The Royal Malta Artillery as Anti-Aircraft Gunners. The Regiment was stationed in Malta until March, 1944, with the distinction of sharing in the defence of the fortress during the whole siege, from 1940 until 1943, and had a proud record of action during the "blitzes" of 1941 and 1942.

The distinctive badge worn by the Regiment on the battledress sleeve—a Maltese Cross in old gold outlined in red and set on a black shield—was designed by the C.R.A. Malta, who authorized it to be worn by the regiment to commemorate its close association with the George Cross Island and its service, in the late war, in its defence.

24TH HEAVY ANTI-AIRCRAFT REGIMENT, ROYAL ARTILLERY

This Regular regiment traces its origin to the 35th Searchlight Regiment, R.A., which was originally the 35th (First Surrey Rifles) A.A. Battalion, R.E. (T.A.), formed in 1935 by the conversion of the 21st London Regiment (First Surrey Rifles) (T.A.).* It was in March, 1942, that the 35th S.L. Regiment, R.A., was converted to a Light A.A. Regiment, R.A., and renumbered 129. To mark this change the regiment adopted a distinctive flash: a dark-green 2-in. square divided diagonally by a ½-in. scarlet strip. The colours were the old regimental colours of the First Surrey Rifles, which, although forming part of the corps of the East Surrey Regiment, was a rifle regiment wearing a uniform with facings similar to those of the King's Royal Rifle Corps. The 129th L.A.A. Regiment served in Burma with the Fourteenth Army, and there is a theory that the regimental flash was designed to represent the flash of a Bofors gun against the green of the jungle, but

* Raised in Camberwell in 1859 as the 1st Surrey Rifles.

it is felt that the association of the regiment with the First Surrey Rifles is the real reason for the adoption of the colours.

In 1947 the 129th Light A.A. Regiment was renumbered 24, and in 1948 it was converted into a Heavy A.A. Regiment.

The regimental flash is worn only on the left arm below the A.A. Command badge.

297TH (KENT YEOMANRY) LIGHT ANTI-AIRCRAFT REGIMENT, ROYAL ARTILLERY (T.A.)

This regiment descends from the Royal East Kent Yeomanry (The Duke of Connaught's Own) (Mounted Rifles) and the West Kent Yeomanry, which were amalgamated in 1920 and converted to Royal Artillery as the 97th (Kent Yeomanry) Field Brigade (later Regiment) R.A. (T.A.).

The Royal East Kent Yeomanry had as their badge the white horse of Kent above a scroll bearing the motto "Invicta," set within a garter surmounted by a crown, below the garter a scroll on which was the inscription "Royal East Kent Mounted Rifles"; whilst that of the West Kent Yeomanry was again the white horse of Kent set on a scroll bearing the word "Invicta," surmounted by a crown and the inscription "West Kent (Queen's Own) Yeomanry" on a scroll.

The regiment now wear the Royal Artillery cap-badge, but to retain their Kent Yeomanry traditions and associations wear on the left arm a black diamond, on which is the white horse of Kent.

402nd LIGHT REGIMENT, ROYAL ARTILLERY (ARGYLL AND SUTHERLAND HIGHLANDERS) (T.A.)

This regiment traces its origin to the 5th and 6th Territorial Army Battalions of the Argyll and Sutherland Highlanders. In 1941 these two battalions were converted into the 91st and 93rd Anti-Tank Regiments, R.A. Reformed in 1947 as the 402nd Anti-Tank Regiment, R.A., it became a Light Regiment, R.A., in 1949. Although gunners, the regiment wears the Balmoral bonnet with the cap-badge of the Argyll and Sutherland Highlanders and wears the regimental flash on the arm below the formation badge. The flash, 2 in. long by ½ in. deep, has two narrow dark green edges and red and white dicing.

515th (ISLE OF MAN) LIGHT ANTI-AIRCRAFT REGIMENT, ROYAL ARTILLERY (T.A.)

This Territorial Army regiment was raised in 1938 as the 15th (Isle of Man) Light A.A. Regiment. On the re-formation of the T.A. in 1947 it was re-numbered "515." This regiment of Manxmen proudly wears a regimental badge below the formation sign, the badge being appropriately the Manx coat of arms, in yellow picked out in black on a red shield.

556TH (EAST LANCASHIRE) HEAVY ANTI-AIRCRAFT REGIMENT, ROYAL ARTILLERY (T.A.)

The red rose of Lancashire picked out in dark blue, with a yellow centre, and five small green petals, set within a white circle—symbolizing the muzzle of a gun—on a dark blue square is the regimental badge of the 556th (East Lancs) Heavy Anti-Aircraft Regiment, R.A. (T.A.), which is worn to link the regiment's association with Lancashire since the early days of the Volunteer Force.

The regiment descends from the Church and Burnley Batteries of the 6th (Lancashire) Volunteer Artillery. After the 1914-18 War these batteries formed the 93rd (East Lancashire) Army Field Brigade, R.A. (T.A.). The regiment was converted in 1938 to a Light A.A. Regiment —52nd—and on the re-formation of the Territorial Army in 1947 assumed its present role and title.

573RD (MIXED) HEAVY ANTI-AIRCRAFT REGIMENT, ROYAL ARTILLERY (T.A.) (THE KING'S REGIMENT)

This regiment descends from the 6th (Rifle) Bn. The King's Regiment, which was converted in 1938 to the 38th (The King's Regiment) Anti-Aircraft Battalion, R.E. In 1940 it became the 38th Searchlight Regiment, R.A. In January, 1945, it was redesignated 635th (The King's Regiment) R.A., and re-formed on the reconstitution of the Territorial Army in 1947 as the 573rd (The King's Regiment) (Mixed) H.A.A. Regiment, R.A. (T.A.), the regiment's present title being assumed in 1950.

To link the regiment's descent from the original 6th (Rifle) Battalion of the King's, a regimental badge is now worn on the battledress sleeve. This consists of stringed rifle bugle suspended from the Lancastrian rose. The design is in black set on a scarlet rectangle.

575TH (THE SHERWOOD FORESTERS) LIGHT ANTI-AIRCRAFT REGIMENT, R.A. (T.A.)

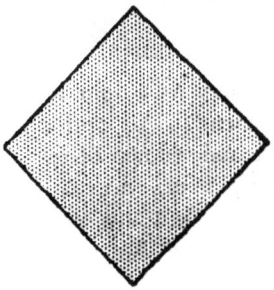

This regiment descends from the 6th Bn. The Sherwood Foresters (T.A.), which was converted and became the 40th (The Sherwood Foresters) A.A. Battalion, R.E., in 1937. In 1940 it became the 40th Searchlight Regiment, R.A., and in 1945 the 149th (The Sherwood Foresters) Light A.A. Regiment, R.A. It was re-numbered 575 on the re-formation of the Territorial Army in 1947.

The distinctive flash of this regiment is a diamond-shaped piece of grass-green cloth (2 in. by 2 in.) which is worn on the back of the battledress blouse, the apex of the diamond being 1½ in. below the centre seam of the collar. The origin of this flash dates back to the 1914-18 War, when several battalions of the regiment were serving together and it was decided to distinguish the battalions by green flashes cut in different shapes, that of the 6th Battalion being a green diamond.

576TH (MIXED) LIGHT ANTI-AIRCRAFT, SEARCH-LIGHT REGIMENT, ROYAL ARTILLERY (T.A.)

This regiment traces its origin to the 5th Bn. North Staffordshire Regiment (T.A.), and is permitted to wear a flash of the regimental colours of the North Staffordshire Regiment, 2 in. by $\frac{1}{2}$ in., divided vertically into three equal strips—maroon, black and white. The 5th Battalion was converted in 1938 to an Anti-Aircraft Battalion, R.E.—the 41st—becoming the 41st Searchlight Regiment, R.A., in 1940. It was re-formed with its present number as an L.A.A. Regiment in 1947.

580TH LIGHT ANTI-AIRCRAFT REGIMENT, ROYAL ARTILLERY (T.A.)

This regiment is descended from the 5th Bn. The Royal Warwickshire Regiment (T.A.) and continues to wear the crimson horizontal flash which was adopted for identification purposes in 1916 when the 5th, 6th, 7th and 8th Battalions of the regiment were brigaded together.* The 5th Royal Warwicks became on conversion in 1938 the 45th (Royal Warwickshire Regiment) A. A. Battalion, R.E., and in 1940 the 45th Searchlight Regiment, R.A., which in January, 1944, became the 122nd Anti-Tank Regiment. The regiment was re-formed as a L.A.A. Regiment on the re-constitution of the T.A. in 1947.

* The 6th Battalion wore the crimson flash vertically. The 7th wore a blue flash vertically, and the 8th a blue flash horizontally.

587TH LIGHT ANTI-AIRCRAFT REGIMENT, R.A. (QUEEN'S EDINBURGH ROYAL SCOTS) (T.A.)

Official permission was granted in 1951 for this regiment to wear a black thistle on the sleeves of battledress. The badge commemorates the original unit of the Volunteer Force from which this regiment is descended—the City of Edinburgh Volunteer Corps—which was raised in 1859.

In August, 1860, the Corps was reviewed by Queen Victoria, and it was on this occasion that the regiment gained the nickname the "All Blacks" from their dark clerical grey all-black uniform. In 1865 the unit was redesignated the Queen's City of Edinburgh Rifle Volunteer Brigade, which in 1908 on the formation of the Territorial Force became the 4th and 5th Battalions of the Royal Scots. In 1922 the Battalions were amalgamated as the 4th/5th Bn. The Royal Scots (Queen's Edinburgh). The battalion was converted into an A.A. Battalion R.E. in 1938, and in 1940 became the 52nd Searchlight Regiment (Queen's Edinburgh Royal Scots), R.A., being converted to a Light Anti-Aircraft Regiment (the 130th) in 1942.

With the re-formation of the Territorial Army in May, 1947, the regiment was reconstituted with its present title.

602nd HEAVY ANTI-AIRCRAFT (WELCH) REGIMENT, ROYAL ARTILLERY (T.A.)

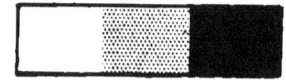

The 602nd Heavy Anti-Aircraft Regiment are descended from the 6th Bn. The Welch Regiment (T.A.), which was converted in 1938 from infantry to gunners to become the H.A.A. Regiment, R.A. (T.A.).

This regiment continues to wear a flash of Welch Regiment colours below the formation badge. The flash is 2 in. long by ¼ in. deep, evenly divided vertically into three divisions—white, red and green.

This flash dates back to October, 1914, when Lady Ninian Crichton-Stuart, the wife of the Commanding Officer, presented each man with this regimental ribbon, which was sewn on to the shoulder of the service-dress jacket as a distinguishing mark in action.

629TH LIGHT ANTI-AIRCRAFT REGIMENT, ROYAL ARTILLERY (T.A.)

Formed in May, 1947, from the 1st Bn. The Cambridgeshire Regiment (T.A.), this regiment is authorized to wear a quarter of an inch below the formation badge, a flash of regimental colours, 2 in. wide and ¼ in. deep, divided horizontally into two strips—Cambridge blue and black.

THE TYNE ELECTRICAL ENGINEERS

The Tyne Electrical Engineers trace their origin to the Tyne Volunteer Submarine Miners (*circa* 1860). This unit later became Electrical Engineers, Tyne Division (Tyne Electrical Engineers); then the Northumberland Fortress R.E.—Tyne Electrical Engineers (Fortress R.E.), from which was formed the 307th (Tyne) Anti-Aircraft Searchlight Company, R.E. (T.A.). This grew into the 37th A.A. Bn. R.E., which was converted in 1940 into the 37th Searchlight Regiment, R.A. The following units trace their origin to the Tyne Electrical Engineers: 537th (M) L.A.A./S.L. Regiment, R.A. (T.A.); 128th Independent E. and M. Squadron, R.E. (T.A.); 104th Army Engineer Regiment, R.E. (T.A.) and the 86th A.G.R.A. Workshop, R.E.M.E. (T.A.), all of which wear the badge of the Tyne Electrical Engineers depicted above—adapted from the crest of the arms of the Board of Ordnance,* the badge being in yellow on a black square.

---

* See page 216.

23RD CORPS SIGNAL REGIMENT, ROYAL SIGNALS (T.A.)

This Territorial unit continues to wear the 1914-18 Divisional Sign of the 47th (2nd London) Division (T.F.). A white eight-pointed star picked out in black and set on a black circle superimposed on a blue square with a narrow black border.

When the Division was re-formed as a Territorial Army formation after the First World War, all units continued to wear the badge. The 47th Division, together with the 56th (1st London) Division, were, however, disbanded in 1935, a large proportion of the infantry battalions having been converted to A.A. Regiments R.A. and A.A. (Searchlight) Battalions R.E. to meet the increasing demands for Anti-Aircraft Defence Units.*

The 47th (2nd London) Divisional Signals on the disbandment of the Division became the London Corps Troops Signals and served as Corps Troops during the late

---

* These units came under command of the 1st Anti-Aircraft Division, the remaining, Field Force units, being grouped into the London Division; the 47th and 56th Divisions being revived in 1939 when, in common with the whole of the T.A. Field Force, the London Division was duplicated.

war. They continued to wear the old 47th Divisional formation badge and retained it when the unit was re-formed in 1947.

THE SUFFOLK REGIMENT

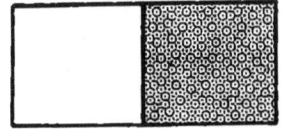

A flash of regimental colours, 2 in. in length, ¾ in. in depth, evenly divided into equal portions of red and yellow, is worn by the Suffolk Regiment.

THE BEDFORDSHIRE AND HERTFORDSHIRE REGIMENT

A flash of regimental colours, 3 in. in length by ¾ in. in depth, is worn by the Bedfordshire and Hertfordshire Regiment below the formation badge. The flash is evenly divided into three vertical strips—black, amber and black.

THE ROYAL SCOTS FUSILIERS

A piece of the Hunting Erskine tartan, cut in the shape of a fusilier grenade, is worn on each sleeve of the battledress by the Royal Scots Fusiliers.

Until 1951 the regiment wore the 42nd tartan (depicted above) and in order not to waste material each was of a different pattern, as the grenades were cut out of lengths of this tartan.

The regiment had, after the 1939-45 War, adopted the Hunting Erskine tartan, the family tartan of the Earl of Mar and Kellie, descendant of the first Colonel of the Regiment, the Earl of Mar.

The regimental pipers wear the Dress Erskine tartan, having adopted this in 1928 to mark the regiment's 250th anniversary.

THE BORDER REGIMENT

In April, 1951, the wearing of this badge was authorized for wear by the Border Regiment, and took the place of the normal Infantry printed shoulder title. It incorporates the title of the regiment in yellow—the colour of the regimental facings—above a yellow glider, set on a maroon background, the maroon being the colour of Airborne Forces.

This badge was introduced to commemorate the first airborne operations by British troops—in Operation "Husky" on 10th July, 1943, the invasion of Sicily. The airborne landing was carried out by the 1st Air Landing Brigade (commanded by Brigadier P. H. W. Hicks, D.S.O., M.C.), then composed of the 1st Bn. The Border Regiment, 2nd Bn. The South Staffordshire Regiment* and the 1st Glider Pilot Regiment.*

---

* A similar badge, with change of regimental titles, has been authorized for wear by these two units—see pages 152 and 153.

THE SOUTH STAFFORDSHIRE REGIMENT

The 2nd Battalion of the South Staffordshire Regiment formed part of the 1st Air Landing Brigade of the 1st Airborne Division in the invasion of Sicily in July, 1943. This was the first occasion on which British glider-borne troops took part in a major tactical operation, and in commemoration of this the South Staffordshire Regiment, in common with The Border Regiment and the Glider Pilot Regiment, now wear a distinctive shoulder title as depicted above, a yellow glider on a maroon ground, with the regimental title "South Stafford," also in yellow.

THE NORTHAMPTONSHIRE REGIMENT

A strip of black cloth 1¾ inches long and ⅜ inch deep is worn on both arms on the battledress sleeve (below the formation badge) by all ranks of The Northamptonshire Regiment.

THE WILTSHIRE REGIMENT

The Wiltshire Regiment wear on the battledress sleeve a small cross pattee of maroon cloth, 1¼ in. in width, the cross being identical with that of the regimental cap-badge.*
This was first worn on the pugarees or topees when the regiment was serving prior to 1939 in India, and introduced for wear on battledress during the late war.

THE GLIDER PILOT REGIMENT

It was the 1st Glider Pilot Regiment which carried the 1st Bn. The Border Regiment and the 2nd Bn. The South Staffordshire Regiment (together with the 9th Airborne

---

* Between 1874 and 1881 the Wiltshire Militia wore a Maltese cross in their badge, which may have influenced the choice of badge for the 1st and 2nd Battalions—the 62nd and 99th Foot respectively—when they became, in 1881, The Wiltshire Regiment (Duke of Edinburgh's).

Squadron, Royal Engineers) into the first glider-borne action by British troops, in the invasion of Sicily in July, 1943; and a similar commemorative shoulder-title badge to those granted to the Border Regiment and the South Staffordshire Regiment was granted* to the Glider Pilot Regiment, the Glider and regimental title being in dark blue on a bright blue background.

* Army Order No. 3 of 1950.

21ST S.A.S. REGIMENT (ARTISTS) (T.A.)

This regiment, raised in 1859 as the Artists Rifles,* became a unit of the Army Air Corps as the 21st Battalion Special Air Service Regiment (Artists Rifles) (T.A.) in 1947. The regiment contrives to wear as its cap-badge the Mars and Minerva badge of the Artists Rifles, but also wears as an arm badge the Special Air Service Regiment's cap-badge—a winged dagger (in white edged with red) striking downwards, light blue wings edged with red, and a light blue scroll, also with a narrow red edge, on which in black letters is the motto "Who dares wins." The design is set on a dark blue background.

---

* 20th Middlesex Rifle Volunteers.

THE MALAYAN SCOUTS

This S.A.S. (Special Air Service) unit, raised in 1951 in Malaya, adopted as its distinguishing badge a white dagger, with blue wings outlined in white, set on a black shield with a narrow white border; above the dagger on a white scroll in black letters the words "The Malayan Scouts," and below the letters "S.A.S." in white. The unit also adopted as a special shoulder title the words "S.A.S. Regiment" and below "Malayan Scouts" in light blue, set on a maroon background.

Miscellaneous Badges

SPECIALIZED ARMOUR TRAINING ESTABLISHMENT, R.A.C.

This Royal Armoured Corps Training Establishment has adopted the war-time badge of the 79th Armoured Division—a bull's head with black and white markings, red and brown nostrils and red-tipped horns set on a yellow background on an inverted equilateral triangle, within a narrow black border. The 79th Armoured Division was a specially equipped assault formation, its armoured units being equipped with special A.F.Vs. and assault devices. It is appropriate that this present-day establishment should have retained this famous war-time badge.

THE ARMY MECHANICAL TRANSPORT SCHOOL

This badge adopted by the Army M.T. School is not worn other than by the instructional staff, and then only on the right breast of overalls. It is, however, used as a vehicle marking and on printed matter. The badge consists of the Imperial Crown in yellow (gold) surmounted by a crowned lion, set above a wheel in red with four yellow spokes and a red hub, the whole on a black shield.

ARMY MECHANIZED DEMONSTRATION COLUMN

This was the column, made up of all arms, which toured the U.K. in the summer of 1946, to give recruiting demonstrations for the post-war army. Personnel of the column wore a rectangular badge evenly divided, top red and lower half dark blue; on it were the yellow letters "AMDC."

BRITISH MILITARY MISSION TO GREECE

The illustration depicts the badge suspended from the short leather thong.

Members of the British Military Mission to Greece wear a special distinguishing badge which, unlike other formation badges, is not worn on the sleeve but is suspended on a short leather thong affixed to the button of the right breast pocket. The badge, one inch wide and two inches in depth, is the Royal Arms of Greece—a shield bearing five light blue and four white vertical stripes below a white cross on pale blue surmounted by a crown.

BRITISH SERVICE MISSION TO BURMA

A Burmese dragon, the Chinthe (pagoda custodian), in white on a red square is the badge of the British Service Mission to Burma. It has a similarity to the wartime badge of the Twelfth Army, which was formed in Burma in May, 1945, and wore a Chinthe in white and gold on a background of three evenly divided bands—red, black and red.

DANISH BRIGADE GROUP

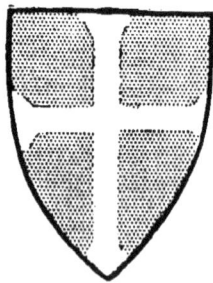

The Danish national emblem, the White Cross or Dannebrog, on a red shield, is the badge worn by the Danish Brigade Group in the British Zone of Germany.

The wearing of Badges on Battledress

The following is the order in which titles and badges are worn on the battledress* sleeve. Firstly, the shoulder title (or tartan flash of Scottish regiments), which is worn on both sleeves. Next, if the wearer is so qualified, on the right sleeve, the Parachute badge with wings,† or the Special Air Service badge. Then, on the left sleeve only, the Infantry Group badge,‡ next the formation badge, which is worn on both sleeves; and then any special regimental flash or badge.

In the Royal Armoured Corps, the R.A.C. Army badge§ is worn by all other ranks on the left upper arm immediately below the formation badge. Officers and other ranks of The Royal Tank Regiment wear the Tank arm badge¶ (in addition to the R.A.C. arm badge) on the right upper arm below the formation badge.

Badges of rank and appointments follow next on the upper arm of the sleeve, and then on the forearm tradesmen's badges.

---

* See pages 162-165.   † See page 196.   ‡ See pages 72-77.
§ See page 129.   ¶ See page 134.

The regimental badge* of the 4th/7th Royal Dragoon Guards worn above a Sergeant's chevrons on the left sleeve, below the small white triangle formation sign of the 1st Division.† Brass shoulder titles are worn on the shoulder straps.

The right sleeve of a Sergeant of the 4th/7th Royal Dragoon Guards with the regimental badge in white metal on a circle of black cloth, above the chevrons.

* See page 131. † See page 54.

BADGES ON BATTLEDRESS 163

Badges worn by a Corporal of the 10th Royal Hussars, with the regimental badge in white metal above the chevrons and below the formation badge, that of the 2nd Infantry Division.

The battledress sleeve of a Trumpet-Major of the 14th/20th Hussars, showing the brass shoulder title on the shoulder strap, the crossed kukri badge,* the formation badge of the 3rd Infantry Division, and the badge and chevrons of the appointment on the forearm.

* See page 133.

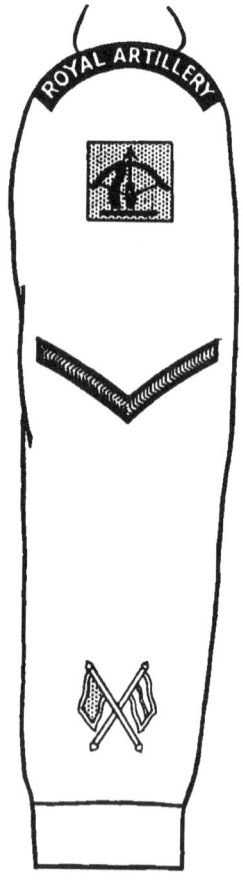

The sleeve of a Lance-Bombardier Signaller, Royal Artillery, of a unit of Anti-Aircraft Command, the shoulder title, red lettering on blue, the A.A. Command formation badge, the single chevron denoting the Non-Commissioned rank, and the Signaller's badge on the forearm.

The badges of a Sergeant of the Royal Engineers, the R.E. grenade below the formation badge and above the three chevrons.

BADGES ON BATTLEDRESS 165

The battledress sleeve of a Company Quartermaster-Sergeant of the Parachute Regiment, with the Regular Parachute troops badge below the regimental shoulder title and above the Airborne Forces badge.

The badges of a Band Corporal of the Royal Hampshire Regiment below the Wessex Group badge.*

* See page 74.

BATTALION NUMERALS

Each battalion of the Coldstream Guards is distinguished by the wearing of a battalion numeral in scarlet cloth sewn on the sleeve of pre-war service dress and now battledress, below the shoulder title and above the formation badge (when this is worn).

The figure is a Roman numeral I for the 1st Battalion, II for the 2nd and III for the 3rd.* The numerals of the 1st Battalion are 1½ in. in length by ⅜ in. wide, as are also those of the 2nd Battalion, which are sewn to the sleeve separately but in the case of the 3rd Battalion the numerals are conjoined as indicated in the illustration below.

This custom was adopted during the latter years of the 1914-18 War and is a custom of dress which does not obtain in the other four regiments of The Brigade of Guards.

* During the 1939-45 War Roman numerals IV and V were worn by the 4th and 5th Battalions.

Tartan Flashes and Patches worn by Scottish Regiments

These tartan flashes and patches are worn on the sleeve of the battledress blouse below the shoulder strap.

THE ROYAL SCOTS (THE ROYAL REGIMENT).—A square ($2\frac{1}{2} \times 2\frac{1}{2}$ in.) of Hunting Stewart tartan.

THE ROYAL SCOTS FUSILIERS.—A piece of Hunting Erskine tartan cut in the shape of a Fusilier grenade (see page 150).

THE KING'S OWN SCOTTISH BORDERERS.—A square of Leslie tartan (2×2 in.).

THE CAMERONIANS (SCOTTISH RIFLES).—An equal-sided diamond of Douglas tartan.

THE BLACK WATCH (ROYAL HIGHLAND REGIMENT).—A piece of 42nd tartan cut in the shape of the star of the Order of the Thistle, which is the background to the regimental badge.

THE HIGHLAND LIGHT INFANTRY (CITY OF GLASGOW REGIMENT).—A patch ($1\frac{3}{4}$ in. square) of Mackenzie tartan.

THE SEAFORTH HIGHLANDERS (ROSS-SHIRE BUFFS, THE DUKE OF ALBANY'S).—A patch of Mackenzie tartan (3 in. wide by $1\frac{3}{4}$ in. deep).

THE GORDON HIGHLANDERS.—A strip ($6\frac{1}{2}$ in. long by 1 in. deep) of Gordon tartan. This strip being sewn around the top of the battledress blouse sleeve close to the seam of the shoulder strap.

THE QUEEN'S OWN CAMERON HIGHLANDERS.—A strip ($3 \times 1\frac{1}{4}$ in.) of Cameron of Erracht tartan.

Officers' Rank Badges

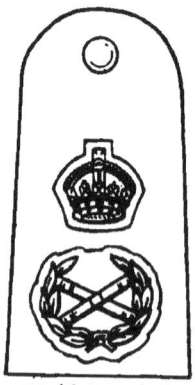

Field-Marshal
Crossed batons with a wreath below a crown.

General
Crossed sword and baton below a crown and star.

Lieutenant-General
Crossed sword and baton below a crown.

Major-General
Crossed sword and baton below a star.

BADGES ON BATTLEDRESS 169

Brigadier
A crown and three stars set in the form of a triangle.

Colonel
A crown and two stars.

Lieutenant-Colonel
A crown and a star.

Major
A crown.

Captain
Three stars.

Lieutenant
Two stars.

Second Lieutenant
One star.

Distinguishing Colouring of background of Worsted Badges of Rank worn on Battledress

RED:	General Staff Royal Army Ordnance Corps Royal Military Police Military Provost Staff Corps Royal Pioneer Corps Royal Artillery
ROYAL BLUE:	Royal Engineers
SCARLET:	Infantry (except Light Infantry and Rifle Regiments)
RIFLE GREEN:	Rifle Regiments
DARK GREEN:	Light Infantry Regiments
EMERALD GREEN:	Royal Army Dental Corps
YELLOW:	Royal Armoured Corps Royal Army Service Corps Royal Army Pay Corps
DULL CHERRY:	Royal Army Medical Corps
BEECH BROWN:	Women's Royal Army Corps

The badges on the battledress of a Captain of the Royal Artillery serving with the 6th Armoured Division, who has qualified as a first glider pilot, and wears the Army Flying badge above the medal ribbons over the left breast pocket.

Gorget Patches

Gorget patches were introduced in 1887 for wear with khaki drill uniforms in India to distinguish General Officers, and certain officers of the Staff and Departments. These patches were symbolic* of the metal gorgets which were a distinguishing feature of officers' uniforms, firstly as a badge of rank and subsequently up to 1830 as an outward sign of the wearer being on duty. These gorgets had their origin in the days of body armour, and were retained as an ornamental survival of the piece of armour which protected the throat (or gorge),† and connected the helmet with the breast and back plates.

The gorget patch as we know it today was introduced in 1896, and was worn on the collar of khaki drill uniforms overseas, and on the collar of the blue serge frock worn by the Staff and Departmental Corps. In 1913 the gorget patch for wear with the open-neck of service dress was introduced. These patches, which became familiarly known as "red tabs," were also worn by all Staff Officers (holding "G," "A," "Q," "MS" and personal appointments) until after the 1914-18 War. In 1921 the wearing of gorget patches was curtailed, and from then onwards they have only been worn

---

* "It is by association of ideas . . . that the term 'Gorget Patch' came about, for there is no actual connection between the piece of armour and the patch of cloth" (*vide* "The Origin and Development of the Gorget Patch," by Major N. P. Dawnay, *Journal of the Society for Army Historical Research*, Vol. XXIV, No. 98, 1946).

† "Military Customs," by Major T. J. Edwards, M.B.E., F.R.Hist.S. (Gale & Polden Ltd., 1948.)

The gorget patch of General Officers.

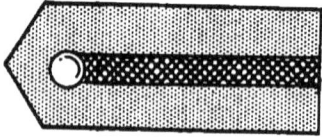 The gorget patch of Brigadiers and Substantive Colonels.

by officers of the rank of Colonel and above. They are worn today in No. 1 dress, service dress and in battledress.

Gorget patches are worn on battledress by Field-Marshals and General Officers, Brigadiers and Substantive Colonels and Officer Cadets.

Those of Field-Marshals and General Officers are 2 in. long, of scarlet cloth, with gilt oak leaves and three acorns.[*]

The gorget patch of Brigadiers and Substantive Colonels is of scarlet cloth with red gimp, and is 2 in. long in battledress.[†]

The distinguishing coloured cloths for gorget patches (which are the same as the cap-band) of senior officers of the various services are:

---

[*] In service dress the gorget patch is 3 in. long and in No. 1 Dress 4¼ in. long and there are four acorns.

[†] In service dress the patch is 3 in. long and in No. 1 Dress 4 in. long.

General Staff Colonels and above: *Scarlet*

Royal Army Chaplains' Department: *Purple*

Royal Army Medical Corps: *Dull Cherry*

Royal Army Ordnance Corps: *Scarlet*

Royal Electrical and Mechanical Engineers: *Scarlet*

Royal Army Pay Corps: *Blue with Primrose yellow welts*

Royal Army Veterinary Corps: *Maroon*

Royal Army Educational Corps: *Cambridge blue*

Royal Army Dental Corps: *Emerald green*

Army Catering Corps: *Pigeon grey*

Queen Alexandra's Royal Army Nursing Corps: $1\frac{1}{2}$ *in. Grey band with $\frac{1}{2}$ in. scarlet cord in centre*

Women's Royal Army Corps: *Beech brown*

White gorget patches, with regimental buttons, are worn by all Cadets at the Royal Military Academy Sandhurst. Cadets at other Officer Cadet Schools wear the Royal Arms button on the white gorget patch.

*   *   *   *

WARRANT OFFICERS, NON-COMMISSIONED OFFICERS SKILL-AT-ARMS AND TRADESMEN'S BADGES

The badges described on pages 176-200 are all illustrated from worsted badges but a number of them are worn in brass.

Rank Badges
WARRANT OFFICERS

Regimental Sergeant-Majors and Superintending Clerks of the Foot Guards

The Royal Arms are worn on the upper arm of the sleeve of battledress, service dress and bush jackets.

Conductors and Staff Sergeant-Majors (1st Class)

The Royal Arms, with the arms surrounded by the garter, and the crown picked out in red and blue, and the supporters in buff thread picked out in black and red, set above two sprays of laurel in buff thread. The badge is worn on both forearms (and may be in brass).

Regimental Corporal-Majors and Farrier Corporal-Majors of the Household Cavalry and Warrant Officers (1st Class)

A printed badge depicting the Royal Arms in its full colours, set on a khaki ground and surrounded by a narrow yellow border. The badge is worn on both forearms (and may be in brass).

Bandmasters

A lyre, surmounted by a crown, set on a wreath of oak leaves in brown and buff thread. This badge is 2¼ in. wide and 3 in. in length. The badge is worn on the forearm of both sleeves of the battledress blouse, service dress or bush jacket. (It may be a brass badge.)

Regimental Quartermaster-Corporals and Farrier Quartermaster-Corporals of the Household Cavalry, Regimental Quartermaster-Sergeants, and Orderly Room Quartermaster-Sergeants of the Foot Guards

A crown set in a wreath and worn on both forearms.*

Squadron Corporal-Majors of the Life Guards

A crown, 1½ in. wide, worn on both forearms.*

Squadron Corporal-Majors of the Royal Horse Guards and Warrant Officers (Class II) of other Corps and Regiments

A crown, 2 in. wide, worn on both forearms.*

---

* The badges may be in brass.

BADGES ON BATTLEDRESS 179

Master Gunners, 1st Class
A gun below the same badge as worn by Conductors and Staff Sergeant-Majors (1st Class), worn on both forearms.

Master Gunners, 2nd Class
A gun below the badge worn by Warrant Officers (1st Class) (the Royal Arms), worn on both forearms.

Master Gunners, 3rd Class
A gun below the badge worn by Regimental Quartermaster-Sergeants, worn on both forearms.

Note.—The badges may be brass or worsted.

NON-COMMISSIONED OFFICERS

Squadron Quartermaster-Corporals and Staff Corporals of the Household Cavalry

Four chevrons, points uppermost, below a crown, worn on both forearms.

Trumpet-Majors of the Household Cavalry

Four chevrons, points uppermost, below crossed trumpets and a crown, worn on both forearms.

Note.—The badges may be brass or worsted.

Trumpet-Majors
Four chevrons, points uppermost, below crossed trumpets worn on both forearms.

Bugle-Majors
Four chevrons, points uppermost, below a stringed bugle, worn on both forearms.

Drum-Majors
A drum above four chevrons, points uppermost, worn on the forearm.

Note.—The badges may be brass or worsted.

Pipe-Majors of the Brigade of Guards

A crown above four chevrons, worn on both forearms.

Pipe-Majors of Scottish Regiments

This badge of four chevrons, points uppermost, below bagpipes is worn by pipe-majors of all Scottish regiments, except the Scots Guards. In this badge the ribbons are picked out in brown thread.

Pipe-Majors of Irish Regiments

This badge* is similar to that worn by pipe-majors of Scottish regiments, except that the pipe ribbons are plain buff thread instead of being picked out in brown as in the case of the Highland pipers. This badge is worn by all pipe-majors of Irish regiments except the Irish Guards.

* See page 188.

Corporals-of-Horse of the Household Cavalry; Squadron, Battery and Company Quartermaster-Sergeants, Colour-Sergeants and Staff Sergeants

Three chevrons below a crown*, worn on the upper arm of both sleeves.

Sergeants (and Band Sergeants of the Foot Guards) (other than R.A., R.E., Royal Signals and Grenadier Guards)

Three chevrons, worn on the upper arm of the sleeve.

Sergeants, Royal Artillery

A gun* above a three-bar chevron is worn on the upper arm of each sleeve.

---

* The badges may be brass or worsted.

Sergeants, Royal Engineers and Grenadier Guards

A grenade,* with seven flames, above a three-bar chevron, is worn on the upper arm of each sleeve.

Sergeants, Royal Signals

The figure of Mercury, holding a caduceus in his hand, poised on a globe—taken from the badge of the Corps—above a three-bar chevron, worn on the upper arm of each sleeve.

Band Sergeants

The bandsman's badge,* the lyre and oak leaves surmounted by a crown, above three chevrons, is worn on the upper arm of both sleeves by all band sergeants except those of the Foot Guards.

* The badges may be brass or worsted.

Corporals and Lance-Corporals of the Household Cavalry and the Royal Gloucestershire Hussars

Two chevrons below a crown,* worn on the upper arm of both sleeves.

Bombardiers (Royal Artillery), Corporals, Band Corporals of the Foot Guards, Lance-Corporals of the Foot Guards and of the 7th Queen's Own Hussars

Two chevrons worn on the upper arm of each sleeve.

Band Bombardiers (Royal Artillery), Band Corporals (except Foot Guards) and Lance-Corporals of the Band and Bugles of the Durham Light Infantry

The bandsman's badge,* above two chevrons worn on the upper arm of both sleeves.

* The badges may be brass or worsted.

Lance-Bombardiers (Royal Artillery), Lance-Corporals (except Foot Guards)

A single chevron* worn on the upper arm of both sleeves.

Band Lance-Bombardiers (Royal Artillery), Band Lance-Corporals (except Foot Guards)

The bandsman's badge above a single chevron is worn on the upper arm of both sleeves. The badge may be brass or worsted.

---

* Lance-Corporals of the Royal Gloucestershire Hussars wear a small crown above the chevron.

BADGES OF APPOINTMENTS

Musicians and Bandsmen (except those of the Household Cavalry and Foot Guards)

The lyre, surmounted by the crown, set on a wreath of oak leaves. This badge is smaller than that worn by bandmasters and is 1½ in. wide and 2 in. in length and is worn on the upper arm of the right sleeve. The badge may be brass or worsted.

Trumpeters

Crossed trumpets in brass or in buff thread, picked out in fawn, is worn on the upper arm of the right sleeve.

Scottish Pipers   *Irish Pipers*

Pipers

Pipers of Scottish regiments, except the Scots Guards, wear the bagpipe badge, the ribbons of which are picked out in brown thread to give the impression of tartan. Pipers of the Irish regiments also wear the bagpipe badge, the ribbons of which are plain. These badges are worn on the upper arm of the right sleeve.

Buglers

A stringed bugle in buff, picked out in fawn thread, is worn on the upper arm of the right sleeve.

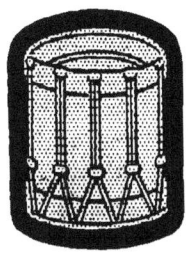

Drummers

A buff drum, picked out in fawn* thread, is worn on the right upper arm. It may be brass or worsted.

INSTRUCTORS

Warrant Officer Instructors, Royal Engineers

The letters "Q.I." above a spray of laurel, and below the seven-flamed grenade badge as worn by sergeants of the Corps, is worn on the left forearm below any other badges. This badge is also worn by qualified instructors in field works below the rank of a warrant officer.

---

* The kettle-drummer of the 3rd King's Own Hussars wears a three-bar chevron on the upper arm of the right sleeve.

Assistant Instructors in Gunnery, Royal Artillery

Two crossed gun barrels in brown thread, picked out in fawn, is worn on the left forearm below any other badges. The badge may be brass or worsted.

Assistant Instructors in Weapon Training

Two crossed S.M.L.E. rifles in brown thread, picked out in fawn and black, worn below any other badges on the left forearm.

Assistant Instructors in Physical Training

Crossed sabres in brown thread with hilts in fawn thread, with hilts picked out in black, worn on the forearm of the left sleeve.

Assistant Instructors in Signalling

Crossed signal flags, one blue, the other white with a blue central line, worn on the left forearm of the sleeve.

Riding Instructors

A spur in brown thread, the rowel and outline in fawn, worn on the forearm of the left sleeve.

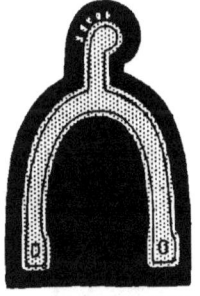

Note.—The badges may be brass and, in the case of the Signaller's badge, the flags may be in enamel.

TRADESMEN

These are worn by all qualified tradesmen so employed, and all are worn on the upper arm of the right sleeve. They are not worn by tradesmen of the rank of sergeant or above.

Farriers

A horse-shoe in fawn thread, picked out in brown and black thread.*

Saddlers, and Harness Makers, and Saddle-tree Makers

A bit in brown thread with its links and curb chain picked out in fawn.*

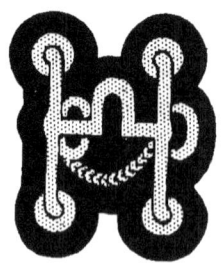

Drivers, Driver Operators and Drivers Road Roller

A white five-pointed star outlined and picked out in black.

---

* The badges may be brass.

Armourers, Blacksmiths, Boilermakers, Engine Fitters, Fitters, Grinders, Instrument Mechanics, Marine Engineers, Millwrights, Machinists, Plumbers and Pipe Fitters, Riveters, Sheet Metal Workers, Vehicle Mechanics and Welders

A crossed pincers and hammer in brown and fawn thread, the head of the pincers and the shaft of the hammer being in fawn thread. The badge may also be in brass.

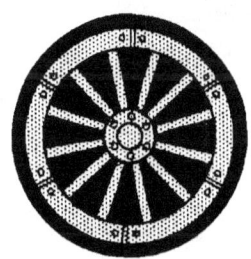

Wheelers, Pattern Makers, Shipwrights, Carpenters and Joiners, Wood Turners and Machinists and Carriage and Wagon Repairers

A printed wheel in black with four brown spokes on a fawn hub.

Ammunition Examiners, Royal Army Ordnance Corps and Assistant Ammunition Examiners, R.A.O.C. (W.R.A.C.)

An embroidered badge, a black circle on which is the letter "A" in yellow, surrounded by five red and thirteen small yellow flames.

Operators, Radio Telegraph and Line Mechanics

A white circle with six white forks of lightning set on a dark blue background.

Telecommunication Mechanic

A red circle with six red forks of lightning set on a dark blue background.

Surveyors, Royal Artillery
   A letter "S" in brown thread within a wreath.

Battery Surveyors
   A letter "S" in white.

Groups A and B Tradesmen
   The Group letters, in Old English style, in white within a wreath with white leaves and brown stems.

SKILL-AT-ARMS BADGES

Parachute Troops (Regular Army)

A white parachute with blue and white wings is worn by all qualified parachutists on the upper arm of the right sleeve below the shoulder title and 2 in. from the point of the shoulder.

Parachutists (other than Regular Troops)

A white parachute is worn on the forearm of the left sleeve.

First Glider Pilots

The Army Flying Badge: An embroidered badge depicting the Imperial Crown in full colouring, surmounted by the crowned lion in gold picked out in black, set between two light blue wings, on a dark blue background. This badge is worn on the left breast above the medal ribbons and/or above the pocket.

Second Glider Pilots

A yellow circle, the letter "G" in yellow in the centre, set between two light blue wings, and a dark blue background.

This badge is worn on the left breast above the medal ribbons and/or above the pocket.

Signallers

Crossed semaphore flags, one dark blue, the other white, divided by a blue line.

Snipers

Two snipers' rifles crossed, the letter "S" set between the apex of the two barrels.

Rifle Marksmen

Two crossed S.M.L.E. rifles in brown thread picked out in fawn and black. This badge is worn by all marksmen except those who are qualified to wear the sniper's badge.

BADGES ON BATTLEDRESS 199

Layers Royal Artillery, Mortar-Men and Anti-Tank Layers

A letter "L" in white, set in a wreath with white leaves and brown stems. This is worn on the right upper arm of the sleeve.

Light Machine Gun Marksmen
  The letters "LG" set within a wreath.*

Medium Machine Gun Marksmen
  The letters "MG" within a wreath.*

* Worn on the upper arm of the right sleeve.

Plotters R.A. and Predictor Numbers in A.A. Regiments, Royal Artillery
  A letter "P" within a wreath.*

Height Takers, 1st Class, Royal Artillery (A.A.)
  A letter "H" within a wreath.*

Range Takers, 1st Class, Royal Artillery
  A letter "R" within a wreath.*

* Worn on the upper arm of the right sleeve.

List of Abbreviations

A.A.	Anti-Aircraft.
A.G.R.A.	Army Group Royal Artillery.
A.L.F.S.E.A.	Allied Land Forces South East Asia.
A.M.D.C.	Army Mechanized Demonstration Column.
B.A.O.R.	British Army of the Rhine.
BETFOR	British Element Trieste Force.
Bn.	Battalion.
B.T.A.	British Troops in Austria.
C.I.G.S.	Chief of the Imperial General Staff.
C.C.G.	Control Commission for Germany.
C.R.A.	Commander, Royal Artillery.
FARELF	Far East Land Forces.
G.O.C.	General Officer Commanding.
G.H.Q.	General Headquarters.
H.A.A.	Heavy Anti-Aircraft.
H.Q.	Headquarters.
L. of C.	Lines of Communication.
L.A.A.	Light Anti-Aircraft.
M.E.F.	Middle East Forces.
M.E.L.F.	Middle East Land Forces.
M.S.	Military Secretary.
O.C.	Officer Commanding.
R.A.	Royal Artillery.
R.A.C.	Royal Armoured Corps.
R.A.O.C.	Royal Army Ordnance Corps.
R.E.	Royal Engineers.
R.E.M.E.	Royal Electrical and Mechanical Engineers.
Regt.	Regiment.
S.E.A.C.	South East Asia Command.
S.M.L.E.	Short Magazine Lee Enfield (Rifle).
T.A.	Territorial Army.
U.K.	United Kingdom.
W.R.A.C.	Women's Royal Army Corps.

The formation sign of Aldershot District in use on a direction board.

On Active Service—Officers of the Argyll and Sutherland Highlanders and the Middlesex Regiment wearing the badge of the 40th Division on their arrival in Korea in September, 1950.

The formation sign in use as a vehicle marking. The sign depicted on this vehicle is that of 100 A.G.R.A. (A.A.) (T.A.)

[Photograph by courtesy of "Illustrated

N.C.Os. of the Corps of Royal Military Police displaying the Western Union Standard which incorporates the badge of the Headquarters, Western Europe Commanders-in-Chief (see page 11).

The formation sign of the 52nd (Lowland) Division in use on a Brigade pennant.

The formation sign (and Regimental Number) incorporated into the Royal Artillery Standard. The Standard illustrated incorporates the badge of 100 A.G.R.A. (A.A.) (T.A.) as flown by 667 Heavy Anti-Aircraft Regiment, Royal Artillery (T.A.). It was in July, 1945, that it was first proposed that there was a need for a flag, of some kind, for units of the Royal Artillery, and this was agreed to by the Master Gunners Committee. A design produced by the College of Heralds was approved by H.M. King George VI. The Standard (depicted above) which was adopted in August, 1947, is elongated in shape to conform to heraldic usage and custom. Formation badges may be included (as illustrated above) in the "field," in the dexter chief angle (the top left-hand corner) above the Regimental Number.

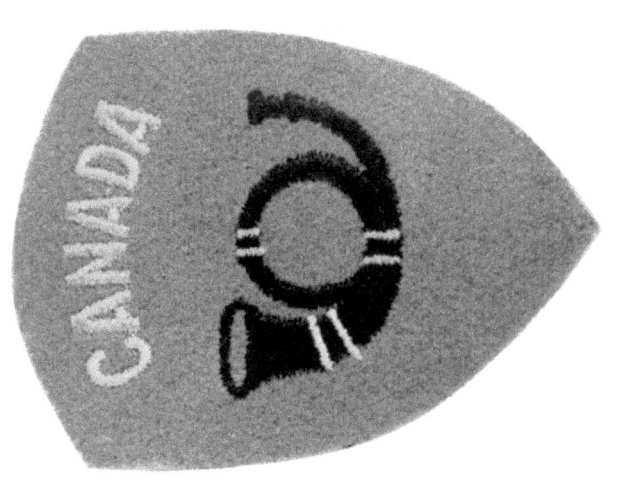

The badges of SHAPE (Supreme Headquarters Allied Powers Europe) and the 1st Canadian Rifle Battalion which forms part of the 27th Canadian Infantry Brigade in Rhine Army. These badges, reproduced in actual size, give an indication of the details of manufacture and of the materials used by American and Canadian Forces.

Examples of Ordnance issues of embroidered badges. These badges—of the East Anglian Brigade and of East and West Ridings Area—are reproduced in the actual size as issued for wear on battledress.

These badges of East Africa Command and the 40th Division are reproduced in actual size to give an indication of the detail of manufacture and of the materials of these Ordnance issues. The material is folded along the dotted lines to ensure even edges and to give a neat finish when the badges are sewn on to the uniform. The material is sometimes folded round buckram or some other stiffener before being sewn to the sleeves, or alternatively press studs are sewn at the back to clip on to the sleeves of khaki Drill Shirts or Bush Jackets which allows them to be detached when the shirt or jacket is laundered.

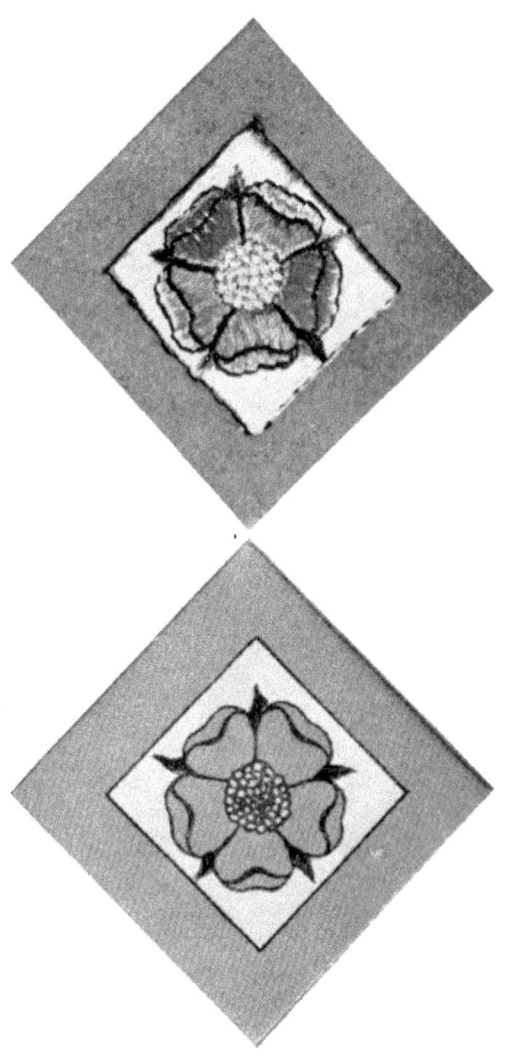

The two types of formation signs as worn. Above, the issue printed sign of the 42nd (Lancashire) Division (T.A.), and, below, the embroidered sign. These signs are reproduced in the actual size of the signs worn on battledress.

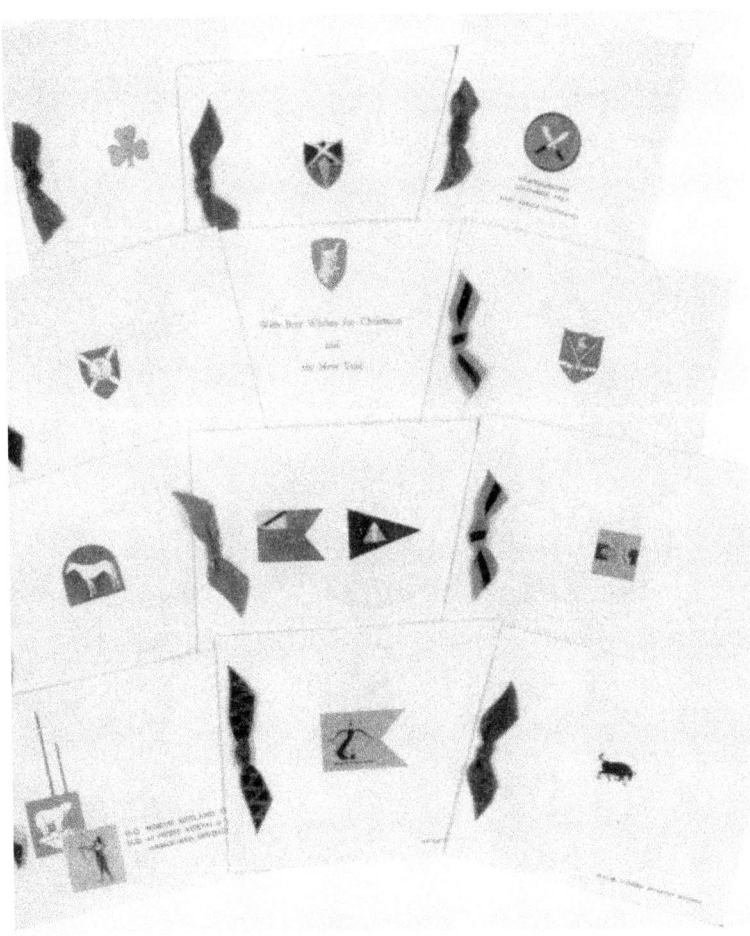

Formation badges in use on Greeting Cards. Illustrated above are Christmas Cards from (left to right—top): 107th (Ulster) Independent Brigade (T.A.); H.Q. Aldershot District; H.Q. East African Command; 264th (Scottish) Beach Brigade (T.A.); H.Q. East Anglian District; H.Q. Eastern Command; 9th Independent Armoured Brigade; H.Q. Canal South District and H.Q. 17th Infantry Brigade (the formation signs set on the District and Brigade pennants); H.Q. Scottish Command; H.Q. North Midland District and H.Q. 49th (West Riding and Midland) Armoured Division; H.Q. Anti-Aircraft Command; and H.Q. 91st Lorried Infantry Brigade.

The use of the formation badge in Command and Divisional Medals and trophies awarded for Athletic and Rifle Meetings and other such events. The badges reproduced above are those of: (top—left to right) H.Q. B.A.O.R.; Far East Land Forces; A.A. Command; Eastern Command; Southern Command; 1st Corps; 7th Armoured Division; Aldershot District; and Home Counties District.

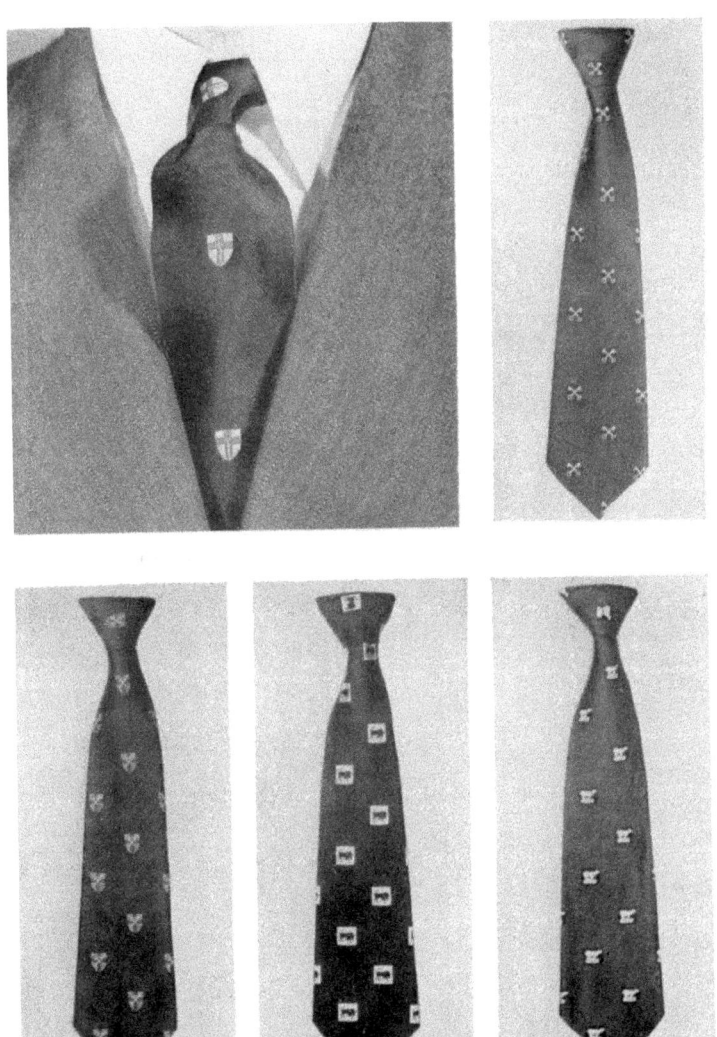

The formation badge in civilian dress. Badges reproduced on ties, and worn by serving and ex-members of the formations. Those depicted above include the badges of: Second Army; 21st Army Group (and H.Q. Rhine Army); 2nd Infantry Division; 11th Armoured Division; and 49th (West Riding) Division (T.A.).

The Arms of the Board of Ordnance.

Metal and worsted badges of Tradesmen and Appointments. Top: Bandsman's badge. Centre: Signaller's (in enamel, worsted and in brass). Lower: Armourers, Fitters, Blacksmiths, etc. (See page 193.)

The badge of rank of a Warrant Officer 2nd Class (Regimental Quartermaster Sergeant) in worsted and brass (reproduced in actual size as worn on battledress).

BADGES ON BATTLEDRESS

Two well-known Formation Signs, those of Anti-Aircraft Command, and our Airborne Forces; and a Territorial Army Formation Sign, that of 100 A.G.R.A. (T.A.), worn by an R.S.M.

www.ingramcontent.com/pod-product-compliance
Lightning Source LLC
Chambersburg PA
CBHW070840160426
43192CB00012B/2255